John

Tamar to Scilly

A life-long Odyssey to the Isles of Scilly

Published in Great Britain in 1997 by
Seabird Publications
Bay Tree Cottage
Old Town
St Mary's
Isles of Scilly
TR21 0NH

Printed and bound in Great Britain by
Peter Howell & Co., The Printing Press, 21 Clare Place
Coxside, Plymouth, Devon. PL4 0JW

ISBN 0 9532052 0 7

To Jon

Tamar to Scilly

One day maybe....?

♡ Jacqui x

Feb. 14th. 1999

Acknowledgments

To those good friends on Tamarside who gave so generously of their time and skills to work on *Fairwater* and the other good friends in Scilly who were always so friendly and helpful. Their names appear in print in the course of the story.

To all the many authors of books on the Isles of Scilly who have given me so much pleasure and information over the years and especially Professor Charles Thomas and Paul Ashbee.

To Rosemary Codd who cheerfully spent the requisite time to process my scribble and present it so efficiently in publishable form and to Peter and Margaret Rowe of The Strand, St Mary's for the artwork on the cover.

To my wife Peggy,
the indispensable crew
who was sadly missed
on the final journey home.

Preface

This is the story of two ordinary people: one the son of a Devonport dockyard worker and one the daughter of a Saltash butcher. They married and both worked hard to build a good home. Their lives were enriched by a mutual love of the sea and sailing. By chance they also fell in love with the Isles of Scilly and the very special Islanders who live there.

As part of the demanding process of running a boat, which is a home afloat, sailing from the Tamar to the Isles of Scilly over a period of over thirty years, log books were kept to record the voyages and as the years went on, experiences were recorded not just in words but in colourful photography.

If only some small part of the excitement of voyaging and the satisfaction of dropping anchor in some much loved harbours can be passed on to readers of this story, then all the effort of the sailing and all the work of writing about it will be richly rewarded.

19.5.97

Chapter One

How easy it is to return to the days of happy childhood when my obsession with boating first began. On a hot Summer day in the early 1930's my parents and a few other close members of the family hired a rowing boat from the Waterside at Saltash. It was a substantial working boat as used by the local salmon fishermen and we took a picnic up river to Warleigh Point, a mile or so up the river Tamar from the Royal Albert Bridge. The sheer height of Brunel's masterpiece made a memorable departure point. The railway track soared over a hundred feet above water level, where the gleaming dark green G.W.R. steam locomotives pulled trains of chocolate and cream carriages taking holidaymakers towards Penzance, through the scenery of the Cornish Riviera. As the engines hissed and barked with suppressed energy, throwing out clouds of dramatic steam and the passengers excitedly looked through the opened windows as they passed over this gateway into Cornwall, we, in contrast, gently pulled away up river making smooth and silent progress through the water.

This was the way that for countless centuries people had travelled to and from the fertile slopes of the Tamar Valley to the growing 'Three Towns' of Plymouth, Devonport and Stonehouse at the mouth of the estuary. Three hundred ton schooners brought coal and timber to the mines in the valley, and bore away the rich, heavy cargoes of tin and copper ore, silver and arsenic won with such labour from the depths of the Tamar Valley mines. Barges carried limestone to the kilns to enrich the soil and brought back to the markets of the crowded Royal Dockyard area the vegetables, strawberries and cherries and baskets of salmon, wrapped in green ferns and eagerly bought by the families downstream.

The railway reduced the traffic on the river. The schooners, paddle steamers and barges became fewer and finally the invading streams of road traffic killed them off altogether. But as a four or five year old boy on a holiday outing I knew nothing of this sad decline of the river traffic. I thrilled instead to the feeling of being afloat, enjoying the rhythmic music of the oars beating through the water and the sight of the green river banks gliding past.

What joy there was on landing on a little beach, paddling in the water and eating the picnic, stretching out on the sand, in the sun, looking over the wide expanse of water running up past Cargreen to the distant twists and turns upstream. Then, on the way home, sad at leaving every child's idea of heaven: a sandy beach (for this is where all life on Earth began, where the

The Royal Albert bridge, Saltash. Vehicles queue for the ferry across the Tamar

sea caressed the land) I trailed a home-made boat astern on a length of string trying not to mourn for the end of a happy day. Then this feeling of gloom changed into a most incredible thrill. The oarsmen now snapped into a racing pace, throwing their shoulders back, striking the water quickly, feathering the oars, to drive the boat upwards and onwards before it lost its momentum from the previous stroke.

My flat little triangle of wood (such was my model boat!) now came to life, its bow lifting in turn, even throwing a bow wave back fast and high, and looking over the transom I saw the flat surface of the river churned into a twisting wake with regular little whirlpools on either side lining up like outriders, outpaced and fading into the distance.

In this scene, in this excitement were the seeds of my obsession firmly planted: the wake astern of the speeding boat; the beckoning river ahead leading to the open sea; the urge to run down channel following at sea the Cornish Riviera Express on its journey to the west towards Penzance and Land's End. I was not to know that beyond the end of the Cornish cliffs lay the ultimate attraction. Twenty five miles to the west lay that circle of silver beached islands where the sun sets over the broad Atlantic, where numberless generations of Celts had entombed their noble dead, as they believed, as close as was possible to heaven. What follows is the story of how this ordinary little boy ended up in these Isles of Scilly, drawn there inevitably by a quite extraordinary life-long Odyssey.

My childhood followed the pattern of most children in the Tamarside area where the Royal Dockyard at Devonport and the Navy based there provided nearly every family's employment. I was a short sighted little scholar who found learning easy and my early ambitions concentrated on getting away from the Saltash Council school at North Road to qualify for the recently built County Grammar School out in the green fields near the adjoining Parish of St Stephens.

The humdrum process of my education was made complicated by the outbreak of World War II in my ninth year. Later with the North Road School having been 'blitzed', I took my 11+ exam after nights in the air raid shelter while Plymouth was systematically bombed to destruction by the Luftwaffe in the Spring of '41.

Amid the gloom of rationed food and clothes, Winter blackouts and travel restrictions, I still saw enough of the river and the sea to keep my interest in them alive. Brief family holidays were possible at Padstow and St Ives and the Tamar was just a short walk downhill from my home. Beaches were still accessible even if boating on the Tamar was banned by wartime restrictions. I used to love wading about in the shallow water, making islands of weed covered rocks, in preference to learning to swim. Much as I loved being on or near the water, trying to swim in it filled me with fear and panic.

In spite of the efforts of the Luftwaffe, the steam driven ferry still crossed beside the railway bridge, both being unscarred by the sticks of bombs which fell in direct line only a few hundred yards to the west and destroyed shops and houses in Fore Street, Saltash. On the ferry's regular crossings, I occasionally enjoyed my right, as a junior citizen of Saltash, to travel on it free of charge watching the Naval small craft rushing past, or leaning over the side to watch the chains clanking on board as the ferry struggled against the strong river currents.

As teenagers, towards the end of the war, we were able to do a little boating by dashing out on our bicycles to Antony Passage on the Lynher river, where dockyard restrictions ended (or were ignored) and where we could hire a rowing boat from the Crossley family who were the local fishermen and ferrymen. Here we learned to row and navigate around the beautiful scenery up river past Ince castle, to where the river narrowed and twisted past Erth Island and the 'Dandy Hole' anchorage on its way up to St Germans. No instruction was considered necessary then, no life jackets were worn, and we never came to any harm.

Even when playing cricket with my pals on the recreation field, which looks over the broad reaches of the Tamar above Saltash, my mind would be dreaming of boats and river banks instead of concentrating on the game. I was once felled by a particularly well struck ball that hit me on the back of the head while I was daydreaming. Not one of the anxious faced lads who lifted me off the ground said I shouldn't have been looking the wrong way, or complained that I had missed a good catch. They all knew that although muscular and agile, my short sight and lack of natural aggression made me quite hopeless at any form of team game involving a ball. Rowing and sailing, however, would be completely different.

To my great delight, as the war in Europe ended and restrictions on the river were lifted, my father bought an eighteen foot sailing boat, which had been laid up and neglected on the Saltash waterfront over the wartime years. Its condition can be surmised from the fact that he bought it for four pounds ten shillings. *Eileen* was her name and she was a fast, lightly built dinghy, probably one of the Jolly Boat class that raced in Plymouth Sound before the war.

My father was well able to repair *Eileen* as he was a highly skilled joiner and furniture maker (as well as compass adjuster) in the Devonport dockyard. He had a small workshop in the backyard at home, where I developed a love for the feel and smell of good quality timber and acquired some basic wood working skills at considerable cost to my father's tools, making model boats to my own outlandish designs when he wasn't around to stop me.

I remember one childish project which had its inspiration in the Trafalgar era, when huge 'Men o' War' such as Nelson's *Victory* blasted all England's enemies into submission. I took a large piece of hardwood and converted it into a ship of the line. The bow was crudely made into a 'V' shape, the stern equally crudely tried to imitate the Captain's cabin and poop deck. I drilled lines of portholes into the sides, more appropriate to the *Titanic* than to the *Victory*. Somehow I fitted it with masts and it was fitted with model guns, quite out of period which could make a satisfying bang with the use of a cap, so easily obtainable then but probably outlawed by Brussels now.

My ship of the line sailed across our sitting room carpet in my childish play. The gun fired with satisfactory noise and gunpowder smoke but it did not fire a cannon ball. How could I make balls to fit the gun? The answer was to collect dribbles of tar from the road and roll them into little balls that would fit into the barrel of the model gun. Against all probability, it all worked. I lay on the carpet, lined up the gun and fired tar balls with great accuracy at all the sitting room furniture.

This game was so satisfying, it could have gone on for ever, but my mother arrived, mercifully in time to clear up the tar spangled furniture before my father returned from work, while I was given the opportunity to hide my 'Man o' War' in the deep recesses of the workshop. I have to admit to an element of madness that still traumatizes and enriches life today, when I should be a much more sober senior citizen than I am.

We learned to sail *Eileen* the hard way, with very little instruction or advice, and thanks to an iron centreplate keel, which could be lowered nearly six feet and good side decks and cockpit coamings, we never capsized her. The seeds of enthusiasm for boating sown in my early childhood now flourished and expanded in all directions.

Eileen, in which I learned to sail. My father and Peggy are the crew.

Sailing is a very tactile experience. My hand on the tiller learned to feel the pull of the water rushing past the rudder. My hands held the sheets controlling the sails and could pull them in or ease them out to command the exact amount of power required to drive my boat through the sea. I could feel the wind on my face and by watching the flurries of the wind over the waves I could compute the wind speed and direction.

There is nothing wrong with the owner of a modern plastic boat detecting these forces by an instrument on top of his mast then relating them to the boat's course on yet another instrument, but all these electronic inventions must interfere with the sheer joy of sailing with the closest possible personal contact with the wind and the sea. With such powerful forces involved, for winds are not always gentle and the frightful power of gale driven waves have to be experienced to be appreciated, the sailor has to treat the sea with the greatest respect. Clever as he is, he is only a minute speck on the surface of the all powerful sea. Can a bird describe the thrill of flight? Can a fish tell what it's like to swim? How can I, as I write this in my sixty seventh year; put into words the joy of sailing, especially as I came to experience it when I was a teenager?

Of course I'll sail:
The Scilly god demands
Before I fail
That one last sail boat's in my hands.

To skim the waves,
To fly across the winds,
To fill the urgent sails,
To leave the land behind.

Sometime, half way before I die,
I'll sail my dream boat to the sky.

When learning to sail *Eileen* I was at first frightened, then fascinated and finally entranced with the whole experience. It took my love of being afloat and rowing boats into a new dimension. The colours of the sails, the sky and the sea; the smell of the cold salty wind and the feel of it flowing over my face, hands and hair; the excitement of the speeding boat and feeling in full control of it: I loved it all with never ending teenage passion.

We had a half share in a council boathouse on Ashtor Wharf, right underneath the Royal Albert Bridge and immediately inshore from the tall bridge pillar that had so impressed me as a child. We had a mooring in deep water a little further up river – off Brunel Green. We had a pretty little clinker built dinghy to take us out to the mooring, big enough to use in the Autumn (when *Eileen* was laid up in the boat shed) for beachcombing trips up river to find branches and planks for firewood for the approaching Winter. We even bought an outboard motor of dubious origin which enabled us to run back in windless conditions in the evenings, after long daytrips sailing past Plymouth Breakwater to Cawsand and back to Bovisand or Jennycliff.

My mother, who devoted her entire life to the needs and whims of my father and myself and consequently was never adequately appreciated, had no great love of boating. When she did try the delights of sailing in *Eileen* with me at the helm, I was so carried away by youthful exuberance and delight in new sailing skills that the boat was driven at extreme angles of heel and only brought about at the last second with the bowsprit nearly touching one of the many warships moored in the harbour. Thereafter she spent hours in the boathouse, knitting and boiling the kettle on an old Primus stove, ready to feed us on our return.

We have found since that one problem with sailing and cruising for most men is that its risks and discomforts do not generally appeal to the best instincts of womankind and this often causes strains on family relationships. How often we have talked to yachtsmen away from home with a crew of friends, whose happiness is overclouded by feelings of regret that half the family has had to be left behind by reluctant mutual consent. More equality between the sexes has no doubt diminished this problem, but I doubt that it will ever go away completely.

As I reached my late teens, any potential problem in this direction was solved for me without any conscious effort on my part. My father, who had a rich baritone voice (which to my regret I did not inherit) was, appropriately enough, playing the part of Captain Corcoran in the local Gilbert and Sullivan production of HMS *Pinafore*. A young soprano in the cast mentioned in casual conversation that, much as she loved boating, rowing and canoeing, she had never yet had the opportunity to go sailing. She was invited to become part of *Eileen's* crew for a day trip on the following Saturday. When this

Peggy sailed and maintained her own 'Whitewing' dinghy. My father stands in the doorway of our boathouse on Ashtor Wharf

news was broken to me midweek, I said that the young lady was only known to me as the objectionable sister of one of my school pals and that I was sure she would spoil our sailing as surely as she plagued the life out of her charming brother at home! How soon can one's prejudices be overcome! Instead of discord, she brought a spirit of sheer joy to sailing. She could row. She could tie knots. She could swim like a fish, she could sit out the boat, with her hands lacerated by the jib sheets, her back aching, frozen by the wind and the spray and still come back to the mooring smiling. She also had the curves, sections and underwater profile that would send a young naval architect into ecstasy. So, little as we both realized it at the time, my future wife Peggy became an integral, and indispensable part of the sailing obsession that stayed with us to the end.

For the next six years my boating activities had to be put on the back burner as the demands of a career intervened. I chose to do my two years national service in the Royal Air Force before going to university for a degree to be followed by training to be a teacher. At that time my achievements at Saltash Grammar School had been so rewarding that there was nothing in the world I wanted to do so much as become a teacher. It says something for the political meddling with education over the following 30 years that at the end of that time there was nothing I wanted so much as to get out of teaching.

My qualifications sent me into the Personnel Selection Section of the R.A.F., thereby sentencing me to permanent residence in recruit training camps, drearily processing other conscripts and never having the satisfaction of seeing a single aircraft take to the skies. Precious weeks of leave in the Summer gave me some sailing and every 48 hour weekend pass I could obtain brought me home to my family, friends and Peggy, who had now become my long suffering fiancée.

I managed to get out of the R.A.F. in 1951, a couple of months early, in order to take up my place on a history degree course at Exeter University. The quality of life increased greatly. I was nearer to home and could travel at weekends economically on the double decker Western National bus which took a leisurely three hours for the journey from Exeter to Plymouth. Lectures were interesting and infrequent and the written work was not too demanding, thus providing that nicest of all commodities, spare time. Some of that spare time was very usefully spent on some small scale boat designing. Meanwhile in my father's shed at home a couple of clinker praam dinghies were built, followed by a strip planked mahogany outboard runabout. It is not surprising that with all these non academic distractions I was lucky to get a degree at pass level at all and the dozen or so final exam papers gave me nightmares of inadequacy for years afterwards. Then along came my teaching career at the time the Labour government was spending money on new secondary modern schools and Plymouth needed new teachers for them, so finding employment was not difficult.

One of the clinker Praam dinghies built in my father's shed to my design

Boats and boating became my main interest in adult life, as it had been in my teens and apart from anything else, teaching conveniently provided three weeks holiday at Easter for fitting out and six weeks in the Summer for cruising.

Fortunate coincidences helped this obsession with sailing to flourish. On a short holiday in Penzance, my parents and I were easily encouraged to go on a day trip to the Isles of Scilly in the Steamship Company's *Scillonian II*. Peggy did the encouraging as she had spent two holidays there, the first in 1947 when she flew over on one of the old De Havilland Rapide biplanes and where she completely fell in love with the scenery, the Off Islands, the boating trips and the beaches where she acquired a spectacular suntan.

The varnished mahogany runabout which was designed to be as large as was possible within my father's shed

I remember nothing of the sea trip, but I remember the arrival amongst this circlet of jewelled islands and the feeling that this place was different from anything I had ever seen before and beautiful beyond belief. We walked on St Mary's and again I remember nothing of the little granite houses and shops of Hugh Town; but I can picture the pale sand, the emerald and sapphire waters of Porthcressa and the great tumbled granite blocks of Peninnis headland as vividly now as when I first saw them that day. The final and fiercest element in my obsession was now complete. I had to sail a boat of my own to these magical Isles of Scilly and learn, if that were possible, to master the channels and tides to visit them all and marvel at their great variety.

This would have remained a dream but for the next coincidence. We were now married (1955), and had put down a deposit and arranged a mortgage on a house overlooking the Tamar at Saltash Passage. We had to sell our dinghies to finance this but the river was just a stone's throw from the bottom of the garden and we enjoyed unrestricted views up and down river and across to the boathouse immediately opposite on the Saltash side. Bus services were handy to my school and Peggy's insurance office. We frequently travelled across the river on the old steam ferry to Saltash and there we met the owner of a 4½ ton Hilliard cruising yacht, a garage owner from Callington, who welcomed our local knowledge and willingness to keep an eye on his boat in his absence and who offered us the chance to crew for him on occasional day trips.

At twenty two feet long, the *Venture* as she was then called, would now pass unnoticed amongst the hundreds of larger G.R.P. boats lying in strings in our part of the river today. But in the 1950's she was a rare example of a seaworthy little cruising yacht. She had a good Stuart Turner auxiliary engine, comfortable bunks for two and a smart little sea toilet forward of the mast, discreetly separated from the cabin by gleaming mahogany varnished doors. Peggy and I loved sailing in her, driving her heavy displacement hull which really came to life in strong winds which would have given our dinghies a frightening time. When at anchor she provided basic cooking and sleeping facilities in a safe, cosy environment.

Vyaj was the first boat in which we sailed to the Isles of Scilly

Here was a boat which, with judicious use of the weather could cruise the channel coast and, one hardly dared to think, could even sail past Land's End and into the Atlantic swells to make her way to the Scilly Isles.

In the 1950s, however, newlyweds with a mortgage to pay just could not aspire to such luxuries. No way could we afford the most humble car, certainly not a T.V. and we only had a washing machine plumbed into our cellar when Peggy sold her own beloved 12 foot 'Whitewing' sailing dinghy to pay for it.

Then our garage owner friend decided that next season

his family and business responsibilities were such that he had to sell his boat and, bless his heart, he named a figure for her that I am sure was based on what he thought we might just be able to afford, rather than what he might reasonably expect to ask for her on the open market. I sold the little mahogany runabout and we found the necessary cash to complete the purchase and became *Venture's* proud new owners.

With the outburst of enthusiasm that goes with new ownership our Hilliard was given a thorough refit. The build up of too many coats of white paint on the hull was causing it to crack and flake off. The paint was burnt and scraped off, the planking smoothed and filled, primed, undercoated and finished in pale blue paint (called 'Yachting World' blue after the distinctive colour of every issue of the magazine cover in those days) and finished with a white boot topping at waterline level to set off the shape of the hull. A grid steering compass (ex R.A.F.), new running backstay levers and a new paraffin cooker for the galley were added. Down below in the cabin the varnishwork now gleamed and set off the new blue covers of the bunk mattresses so well that we felt the boat was really ours now and we decided to mark the fact by giving her a new name.

"You can't do that; it's very unlucky", cried our traditionalist friends. Peggy then found the perfect answer in the word for venture, or "setting out on a voyage" in the old Cornish language, which was spelt vyaj (pronounced vee atch). This locked our boat into our obsession for heading down channel towards Scilly, as the Cornishness of her name should make her feel at home there. Maybe next Summer?

The painting, refitting and improvements occupied all the Spring of 1958 and it was with great excitement that we planned a two week cruise, starting on August 2nd. We were going to learn about coastal cruising in the hard school of experience in the same way that we had learned dinghy sailing in *Eileen*. No sailing schools or R.Y.A. seamanship courses existed in those days and we had no experienced friend to guide us out to sea. *Vyaj* began by giving us our first seamanship lessons a few hours after leaving Saltash, before we even reached the open sea. On the way down river, the overcast conditions produced a squall with strong winds and a downpour of rain so we decided to put a second reef into the mainsail before leaving the shelter of Plymouth Breakwater to head around the Mewstone into the River Yealm. As we were hauling on the reefing halliard, the rope broke, the sail flapped about wildly as the reefs unrolled and the end of the hoist drifted skywards. The mainsail was quickly lowered and we motored back to the shelter of Barn Pool to anchor to do necessary repairs and have some lunch. Lesson No.1, check every rope and shackle before going to sea.

We did have some spare rope with us, so we could make up a new halliard, but it had to be put through the pulley block near the top of the mast. A crew conference, after lunch, decided that someone had to be hoisted, via the main halliard, on the bosun's chair, up the mast and that the strongest and heaviest member of the crew (me) should do the lifting, while the lightest (Peggy) went skywards up the mast to thread the new rope through the block. The procedure went quite well, considering that there was no winch to assist with the lift and that Peggy suffers from incurable vertigo.

The replacement having been made, Peggy gratefully made her way downwards, when, within a few feet of safety, the ropes on the bosun's chair died of old age and she was deposited rather inelegantly, astride the main boom. *Vyaj* was giving lesson No.2. Not only must essential equipment be checked, but odd bits of gear, such as the bosun's chair, which might only be needed once in ten years, must be checked and replaced if in doubt. Neither of us needed anyone to point out the potentially crippling, or fatal, results had the bosun's chair's ropes parted half a minute earlier.

Vyaj then gave us lesson No.3, when we tried to lift the anchor. We found that it had entangled itself in one of the many old chains and steel hawsers left in Barn Pool after its use as a major embarkation point for landing craft bound for Normandy on D Day. The lesson was firstly, always use a CQR type anchor and a chain cable; secondly, when fouled pay out some slack and motor gently, but firmly, in the opposite direction from the way the anchor fouled itself and thirdly, avoid any form of anchor buoying like the plague because it causes infinitely more problems than it solves. We have since observed these three rules for nearly 40 years; we always anchor in preference to picking up a mooring and we have never lost an anchor.

We left Barn Pool at 14:00 with one reef in the mainsail, rounded the Mewstone and anchored in the Pool of the River Yealm, an hour and a half later. Four days of miserably wet and windy weather followed, but we enjoyed the perfectly sheltered conditions afforded by the steep wooded slopes surrounding the Pool. A phone call to the Meteorological Office on Tuesday gave promise of northwest winds for the next day with rain and mist clearing away. On Wednesday morning we were up at 05:30 to lift the dinghy onto the cabin roof, raising sail and anchor and heading out to sea and up channel for Salcombe.

We enjoyed every minute of our steady progress across Bigbury Bay, marking our position on the chart occasionally and checking our distance covered as measured by the ex admiralty Walker log we trailed astern. Bolt Tail with the massive cliffs towering over Hope Cove impressed us and we watched with enchantment the sequence of headlands and multicoloured slopes between them and the surge and spray of breaking seas at the foot of

Bolt Head, before we rounded it to be welcomed into the sandy arms of the Salcombe estuary.

The idea was to head down channel again towards Fowey or Falmouth once we had enjoyed a day or two of the delights of Salcombe's anchorage and picturesque little town. On the very day we arrived the weather reverted to the normal August menu of strong southwesterly winds, with either rain, fog or drizzle, or a combination of all three every day. We endured six days of this, made interesting by chance meetings with old friends ashore, hotel lunches with our parents who came up from Saltash by car and watching the daily dinghy races with frequent capsizes in the hectic weather conditions. We also made friends with people on other small cruising yachts, weather-bound like ourselves.

On Tuesday the 12th, in spite of southwesterly headwinds forecast to be force 5, we left early in the morning to slog our way down channel, but turned back when we saw the lines of breaking wave crests off the cliffs of Bolt Head. Back over the steep seas over Salcombe Bar, disappointed with failure, we anchored again, but as the afternoon brought increasingly strong winds, bordering on gale force, we relaxed and enjoyed a certain smugness at having made the right decision.

On Wednesday we decided to try again as conditions moderated. Before we could get under way fog descended and our intended route down river disappeared completely. Thursday brought back strong winds, with rain and drizzle. Friday brought back the fog but we decided to go anyway, encouraged by the friendly and experienced crew of a larger Hilliard *Lilani* who were heading for Fowey and offered to keep us company. We had just moved ahead when our engine made unpleasant clattering noises and lost its cooling water supply. We did the correct thing and sailed back to re-anchor and find a marine engineer, who spent the afternoon replacing the water pump and its shattered drive. Lesson No.4: get to know your engine, maintain it properly, grease it, love it and you will receive loyal service in return.

Lilani had gone, we had lost another day, but one new friend was pleased with our delay because he was sailing single handed to the Scillies for the first time and could join us next day on our return trip to Plymouth to make use of our local knowledge. By a strange coincidence, our new friend was a Welshman who had given his boat a name in Welsh (meaning something like "in good heart"), hwyl. So two boats of the same size, with owners hoping to reach Scilly one day, both with boats with Celtic names *Hwyl* and *Vyaj* came together in a quite unplanned way for this day's voyage down channel.

The remainder of August and the month of September were taken up with day trips with various friends, up river to Calstock or down river to

Plymouth Sound and Cawsand, to catch a few mackerel. We decided to lay *Vyaj* up in Coombe Creek on the Cornish side of the river while her masts and gear were stored in the boathouse at Saltash. We were determined to spend the Winter on improvements, to put into effect the lessons learned from our first cruise and then we could dream about one more Summer devoted to our ambition to sail to Scilly.

Vyaj laid up for the winter in Coombe Creek, Saltash.

Chapter Two

To Scilly 1959

In spite of busy lives and restricted finances, we set about preparing *Vyaj* for the coming season with all the enthusiasm and determination we could muster. The engine was lifted out, taken home and given a thorough refit in our cellar, with spare parts ordered from Stuart Turner. All the rigging wires were replaced with stainless steel, new technology for 1958! We ordered new cotton sails (before nylon became generally available) from MacKenzie of Sandbank in Scotland to ensure the best of workmanship and had the sails mildew proofed and dyed in a tangerine colour which we preferred to the traditional brownish tan because of its outstanding visibility at sea (ask the RNLI for confirmation!) The last and most demanding project was to re-canvas the decks. As this process is now made obsolete by modern materials it may be of interest to describe how it was done. Firstly all the deck fittings, wooden mouldings around the cabin coachroof sides, the toe rail and rubber mouldings had to be removed and the old canvas peeled off to enable the deck planking to be inspected and stopped and smoothed off. We found a source for the supply of Egyptian cotton deck canvas which was cut roughly to shape and the joins were hand sewn by a sailmaker. The wooden decking was then liberally coated with 'special' marine glue which had to be warmed to spread it, the canvas (slightly dampened to make it stretch) laid on top and then carefully ironed on with a hot old flat iron until the glue could be seen soaking right through the material. This process, if carried out properly, bonded the deck, the glue and the canvas into a strong homogeneous surface which when painted could withstand extremes of heat and cold, sea water, rain water and the wear of boots and shoes. Then all the fittings had to be replaced and any canvas still showing trimmed off. Backbreaking, messy, time consuming work which was richly rewarded by the smart appearance of the finished product.

We invested in a hundred feet of new anchor chain, the first 10 feet being heavier than the original. With numerous other detailed improvements we felt happy with the new standard of seaworthiness achieved and finally we ordered mahogany and oak to make a new purpose built dinghy later in the year.

After a few engine trials and day trips in the Spring we were ready for our first weekend afloat at Whitsun. We followed this with a weekend at Fowey at the end of May and another at Salcombe in the middle of June and three weekends in July at our beloved Newton Ferrers on the river Yealm. All these trips added to our experience and confidence and gave us hours of pleasure in return for the hours of work put in over the Winter. It all made us look forward to our first fortnight's cruise in August, in spite of our unkind treatment at the hands of the weather gods the year before. We did not know it, but the weather gods were to decide to make 1959 the sunniest recorded Summer for 200 years.

When my long suffering wife finished work at her office on Friday 31st July, she was shanghaied on board *Vyaj* without delay so that not a minute of sea going time should be wasted. We sailed down river as far as Barn Pool and anchored for the night, lifting the dinghy on to the cabin top ready for an early start next morning. We were up at 07:00 and headed for Penlee Point, to catch the last couple hours of down channel tide past Rame Head. A gentle offshore breeze gave pleasant sailing conditions, but we had ambitions to reach Falmouth and it would be helpful to arrive before the shops closed for the bank holiday weekend. We threw our purist sailing principles overboard and started the engine, throttling it back to its slowest steady purring position, whereupon our speed almost doubled and we felt we were really making progress. We passed Dodman Head at 13:30 and the wind came abeam and strengthened as it tends to do at midday and we kept *Vyaj* tramping along, with her side decks just clear of the water and the bows dashing the seas and the spray purposefully aside. We had discovered the joys of motor sailing! We were also in new territory and Falmouth Bay stretched endlessly ahead with no easy distinguishing features. How I wished that one day I might feel really at home here and know this Bay like the back of my hand! How satisfying, now that I do, passing the frowning Dodman with Caerhays Castle sheltering inshore of it, then the perfect little fishing cove of Portloe with its Lugger Inn, then Gull Rock, quite an island in spite of its name, with a nasty reef running out to seaward of it and then the sweep of the bay, backed by a patchwork of Cornish fields from Penare Point to St Antony's Head guarding the majestic Falmouth entrance, leading to that most beautiful of anchorages at St Mawes, just past Henry VIII's fairytale castle. The scenery never loses its fascination, no matter how endlessly the years roll by.

Once anchored off St Mawes we went ashore to buy some basic ship's provisions, which included a bottle of wine to accompany the four mackerel caught on the way down, for our evening meal.

A good night's sleep was followed by that well earned reward after a good day's passage, of a "Rest Day". In the course of our enjoyable walks around sunny St Mawes, I found the Harbour Master and asked permission to put *Vyaj* ashore in the harbour for a scrub next day. We put her legs on and let her dry out while we had breakfast at 08:30 and spent the day attracting the attention of the visitors while we cleaned the bottom and gave it a fresh coat of red antifouling paint.

When we refloated in the afternoon, in spite of the arrival of a patch of drizzle, we decided to press on westwards, if only for a few miles, across Falmouth Bay to find the entrance of the Helford river. Our new charts guided us through the hazards of the river entrance and we anchored in what had now become a downpour of rain, in this loveliest of Cornish estuaries which we found devoid of activity because of the weather. We had a tent type cockpit cover which when rigged over the boom made a convenient storm porch entrance to our cabin, so that we could take off our streaming oilskins and leave them outside and then enjoy our cosy dry cabin down below. We looked out through the portholes on what looked ominously like a rerun of our soaking wet Salcombe experience of last year, then, late in the evening as the rain stopped, a Scod we recognised (South Coast One Design) came in to anchor close by and we were soon chatting with fellow members of the Plymouth Corinthian Yacht Club, Tommy and Edith Normington, who had just returned from an uncomfortable night's anchorage in Lamorna Cove on an aborted voyage to Scilly.

What promised to be a dismal evening became a pleasant exchange of visits and the promise of meeting up again next day.

So on Tuesday, 4th August, we went ashore to explore the facilities of Helford village. We shopped at the little village store, we filled a couple of water cans from the village pump and we met up with our friends for a visit to the Shipwright's Arms. At that time the pub was run by a landlord who was an ex R.A.F. officer and it had become the mecca for many of the south coast yachtsmen, many of whom were ex R.A.F. Just inside the bar door was a visiting yachtsmen's book and we signed ourselves in, modestly, among prominent names of the yachting fraternity and we continued to do so for quite a few years afterwards before the Shipwright's Arms became relegated into being one of the usual tourist venues of the holiday industry.

After lunch we put our outboard motor on *Caraan's* dinghy and we did a "Cook's Tour" of Helford, exploring Frenchman's Creek and paying tribute to Daphne du Maurier's French pirate, who could still be there undetected and then on to Port Navas, the mecca of oyster lovers and then up river finally to Gweek. How amazing that 36 years later the estuary still remains almost unviolated, except for the intrusion of the customers of Helford

Passage, with the speedboats and waterskiers who don't always realize what a unique maritime environment they are spoiling.

Wednesday, 5th August, was a jewel of a day. Tommy and Edith invited us out for a day on *Caraan* and we were delighted to accept because apart from anything else, their Scod was twice as big, twice as fast and at least twice more modern than our old boat. We enjoyed a day's perfect sailing weather and Tommy took us from Helford to the Lizard and gave us the essential information on how to treat it: with great respect.

"Go well out to sea from it" said Tommy and he pointed out the reef of triangular rock fins, like the back of some sinister sea serpent, stretching out for a mile into the Lizard tide race. I felt a little shiver of fear along my spine at this first sight of the Lizard, even in ideal Summer conditions. I have since confronted it 66 times, up channel or down and the shiver of fear never goes away.

The next morning, Tuesday 6th August, we resisted the temptation to stay with our friends in the Falmouth area, because the call of the Scillies encouraged us onwards and the weather now seemed settled in our favour. We left Helford at 10:00 in perfect Summer conditions and used our motor sailing technique to take us safely around the Lizard and across Mount's Bay. Crossing Mount's Bay in good Summer weather is like drifting through a sailor's idea of heaven. The land with its crowded roads and little towns trying to attract tourists disappeared in a Summer haze. A few yachts, a few fishing boats and a few merchant ships gently crossed the bay. Then the busy seas of the Channel gave way to the long swell rolling in from the Atlantic. St Michael's Mount, Tater Du, Porthcurnow and Land's End passed by and the stretch of Atlantic ocean between Land's End and Scilly lay in wait. Even in calm weather the gentle Atlantic swells are tormented by the tides rushing up and down the English Channel. Tidal streams run strongly sometimes southwest, then turn north for hours, before rushing back up channel, aggravated by jagged reefs: the Sevenstones, the Longships, the steep cliffs of Land's End and the rocks of the Runnel Stone and Wolf Rock.

Before facing the crossing to Scilly we had the option, presented by the fine weather, of going into Penzance Bay to find an anchorage for the night and we chose to explore that most Cornish of all small harbours, Mousehole. We anchored off the harbour and I took the dinghy in to find the Harbour Master (also Car Park Attendant) to ask permission to lie alongside the quay for the night. I gathered that this was not a routine request, because he scratched his head for a bit and said that last year a French yacht had made the same request and he allocated us a berth beside an iron ladder just along from the crane that lowered baulks of timber to close off the harbour mouth in times of bad weather.

We were conscious that a few locals watched our entrance into the harbour and the difficult manoeuvring to come alongside the quay, in the happy anticipation that we would make a complete mess of it and we saw them stroll away downheartedly because we came alongside the quay, made fast and then put a leg on to sit beside the quay in the greatest of comfort for the night. We also heard words of astonishment and envy from tourists on the quay above us:

"Cor, look, they're making a cup of tea!" etc.

We enjoyed an evening stroll around the little port doing some shopping and watching what happened to be the local version of the Helston Flora Dance before settling down to enjoy a night of calm and quiet with *Vyaj* leaning happily against the harbour wall.

After breakfast and some last minute shopping ashore we left the harbour to motor past St Clement's Island nearby then around the coast past Lamorna and Porthcurno, before setting course for Wolf Rock lighthouse, relying on the motor in the calm conditions.

It was a new experience to have this huge expanse of sunlit sea almost entirely to ourselves. As the Cornish coastline began to disappear in the distance, we felt the Atlantic swell gently heaving underneath us. In the kind weather conditions the swells were far enough apart for *Vyaj* to raise her bow and climb uphill for six or seven seconds and then descend on the other side as she assumed a slightly nose down position. All very soothing and pleasant, but we could imagine how steep these swells would become in bad weather, with short wind driven seas crossing them from one direction, while ground seas caused by the tidal streams might jump in from another, throwing a boat our size about very uncomfortably.

Just off Wolf Rock a northeasterly breeze came in quite strongly which sped us towards the Isles of Scilly which appeared to our great relief, just where we hoped they would be and we came close under the magnificent granite rocks of Peninnis Head, to anchor off Hugh Town at 16:00.

We celebrated our arrival in the islands of our dreams by going ashore before and after tea, but we were very concerned that we must not be caught here by bad weather. So because our barometer began to drop rather rapidly, we decided to shelve any plans to explore the Islands and make our way back to the Mainland as soon as possible while the fine Summer weather lasted. Scilly can be very wild and unforgiving in bad weather and only a very small area of the main harbour is sheltered from all directions and even that area is full of local boats and is subjected to a fast running surge coming in over the shallow sandy bottom. Over the years we have seen many dream holidays turn to nightmares while at anchor in the harbour. August usually produces at least one gale to give a severe lesson in respect for the Atlantic weather gods who rule these islands.

So I have no regrets, looking back, that our first visit was so short. We could be accused of being over cautious, but at least our dreams were not shattered. We saw dawn break at 05:00 as we breakfasted before getting away to an early start. To begin with we sailed along nicely in the same conditions as the previous day and we set course for Wolf Rock lighthouse, with the intention of heading for the Lizard, keeping well away from the coast, making our way up channel on the principle that the shortest distance between two points is a straight line.

We were pleased to see the Wolf Rock lighthouse appear as expected on our starboard bow about 5 hours after leaving and we were delighted with the weather conditions now that we had blazing sunshine and calm seas. Unfortunately, once past the lighthouse, Summer became just too perfect and the breeze died away to a flat calm, leaving our little orange sailed boat sitting in a leaden sea, under a hazy blue sky and a roasting hot sun, making about as much progress as the ancient mariner in the doldrums. The faithful Stuart Turner purred into life and we were soon pushing along nicely at our gentle cruising speed of about five knots. A check on the fuel situation revealed that we would run out of petrol before we reached the Lizard. The alternatives were a) to risk putting ourselves motorless in the dangerous tides off the Lizard and, possibly spend the night drifting up and down the channel shipping lanes, or b) go about ten miles off course to call at Mousehole and buy a jerrycan full of petrol, which would see us safely back to the Helford river.

We made a right angled turn away from our chosen course and headed for Mousehole, where we anchored off the harbour entrance. Then we had to lower the dinghy from its lashings on the cabin roof and I struggled ashore through the weed and sludge of the harbour at low tide. The village was deserted with all sensible people seeking shelter from the pitiless blazing sun and sitting in the cool kitchens of their granite cottages enjoying that most delicious of gastronomic treats, your genuine Cornish pasty! The only garage was, of course, half a mile up the steepest hill in the town and the proprietor had to be fetched from his dinner to put four gallons in our can. Then back down the road in the blazing heat carrying the can which was heavy enough to start with, but became even heavier and more awkward as I rushed downhill, inspired by the urgency of proceeding on our long route up channel.

Our Stuart Turner engine, which ran like a sewing machine once started, had one irritating idiosyncrasy. It just would not start when hot! As I dragged the dinghy back through the harbour sludge and rowed out to *Vyaj*, where the dinghy had to be lifted on board and lashed down, I was convinced that after all my toil and sweat, that the engine would not start anyway. But there was a technique that might help. The two spark plugs had to be removed and the engine turned over vigorously with its handle while the petrol supply was switched off. Getting at the plugs involved removing the cockpit floor boards, but in spite of the tropical heat and the sweat running into my eyes, the routine was followed and when the tank was replenished and the starting handle given a few vicious swings at full throttle, we heard the most beautiful music in the world, the urgent, throbbing, regular beat of an engine ready to labour relentlessly at its task of pushing us back up the Channel to our longed for haven in the river Helford.

We arrived with the evening sun still burning down relentlessly from a cloudless sky at 19:30, just 14 hours from Scilly. After a blissful night's sleep and a late breakfast, Tommy Normington came aboard and invited us to join him in a race around the buoys with the local sailing club. We told him what he could do with that idea and opted instead for a gentle run across Falmouth Bay to St Mawes where we could stock up with milk, bread and more fuel. In the afternoon we drifted back towards Helford, through a heat haze which then turned to fog. We went ashore to the Shipwright's Arms to join our friends and then we were all invited aboard another Scod *Sparklet* which was lavishly equipped and we ended up back on *Caraan* for coffee at one o'clock in the morning.

Our friends left early in the morning in *Caraan* to return to base at Plymouth but we decided to cover only half that distance by heading for Fowey, so we made a leisurely start and sailed along the coast towards Dodman Head in relaxed mood, catching a huge mackerel on the line we trailed astern, now brim full of confidence, pleased with our achievement and sure of a trouble free run homewards.

As we rounded Dodman Head and turned into St Austell Bay we became aware of a change in the weather. Looking astern we could see the heat haze replaced with huge black clouds and the sun disappeared. Simultaneously the first heavy drops of rain fell and the first rolls of thunder became increasingly loud and almost continuous. Dressed in our yellow oilskin suits, the rain poured off us, while squalls of wind pushed *Vyaj* over until her side decks were awash, but the sea remained mysteriously flat under the downpour of rain. At one stage, looking at our compass, I realized that by concentrating on sailing *Vyaj* safely through the squalls, we were now heading 90 degrees off course and we just did not know where we were. We could see the occasional flash of lightning striking the sea not far from us and the thunder crashed around our heads like shell fire. After what seemed like an eternity of these frightful conditions, the wind eased and the thunder retreated, but the rain continued to pour down relentlessly. By now we were quite disorientated and the rain reduced visibility to just a few hundred yards. We had to motor, now that an ominous calm engulfed us and my only logical thought was that if we headed due north, we must eventually sight land somewhere in St Austell Bay. We found a headland that we hoped was Gribben Head marking the entrance to Fowey but after passing it and peering at it in the rain we decided it must be Black Head, involving a 90 degree turn to starboard in the hopes of finding the real Gribben Head which we eventually identified by its daymark, only just visible through the still torrential rain. By this time there was no wind at all, the tide was pouring out through the river Fowey entrance and by Paddy's Law that in some situations everything has to go wrong, our engine began to falter and slow down until we almost stopped. The flood of rain water had penetrated the cockpit floorboards and flooded one of the spark plugs, so that the engine was now struggling on only one of its two cylinders. We were making about 2 knots against a contrary tide of about 1½ knots and the engine was sounding as if it might give up at any minute and let us drift back into the Channel. Meanwhile, the rain continued to pour down on us in a vertical cascade. It seemed to take an hour (and it probably did) to cover the last mile into Fowey harbour, where we found the first available space among the moorings off Polruan and dropped the anchor, peeled off our oilskins and the soaking clothes underneath them and revived ourselves down in the cabin with a change of dry clothing and hot coffee laced with rum. When we looked at our watches it was past 4 o'clock, so the storm had lasted over 4 hours and we had had no lunch.

We made a satisfying meal of our monster mackerel and went ashore to phone our parents from the Fowey Yacht Club. All through the picturesque streets of Fowey, shops and houses were doing what they could to remove floodwater and debris from their ground floors and we returned on board in the evening feeling grateful that the storm had caused us nowhere near the damage sustained by most of the householders along the waterfront at Fowey. That night we were subjected to a second thunderstorm but we were just too tired to take any notice of it.

We remained at anchor off Polruan for 3 more days, while the weather deteriorated to a full gale with heavy rain. We were thrown about for a couple of nights by the nasty swell which runs into Fowey harbour in gale conditions and the wind shrieked endlessly through the rigging and occasional drips came through the cabin hatchway.

It was not until Friday 14th August that the bad weather abated. By the evening sunshine returned and we had a final look around Fowey, followed by an invitation aboard for a drink on *Juanita*, a 7 ton gaff yawl that had weathered the gale at anchor astern of us. Her sole occupant was Mrs. Charles Pears, widow of a well known marine artist, who still sailed single handed in spite of advancing years. The next morning dawned fine and sunny and we left Fowey to head back for Plymouth, being waved on our way by our hostess of the previous night, who made her farewells to us dressed in her pyjamas and happily puffing on her pipe!

We sailed back past Plymouth Sound to our much loved anchorage in the river Yealm, where we established a tradition that we would spend the last night of a cruise there and enjoy a celebratory meal in one of the pubs before using the Sunday to return via the Mewstone to the Sound, the Tamar, our mooring and our home.

This fortnight's cruise covered 225 miles to visit 7 different anchorages. This compares well with the 48 miles and two anchorages of last year. But the crowning glory was that we had reached the Scillies and had returned safely. Oh for just one more Summer's cruise to spend more time there!

Chapter Three

1960

Routine fitting out in the Spring was complicated by two factors. Firstly, we built ourselves a new dinghy which could be unbolted amidships to form two halves which would store one inside the other on the cabin roof. The dinghy was strip planked in mahogany, on steamed oak ribs and looked very smart with two bulkheads under the centre thwart, which were sawn apart after the boat was built and then fixed together with two robust brass bolts, with butterfly nuts. It was possible to launch the larger aft section first and then get in it to bolt on the front half, giving us a dinghy several feet longer than a conventional one, which would fit on our cabin roof when passage making at sea. The second complication was a stomach ulcer which gave me great pain and little sleep at night. With our friendly Doctor's help we tried many treatments, bland diets and regular mealtimes, none of which really went with cruising in a small boat at sea.

Nevertheless we had a good Whitsun cruise to Falmouth and a two week Summer holiday going to Salcombe again and then down channel to Helford and Falmouth. We had more day trips than ever, taking a large number of friends and relatives out to enjoy fishing outside Plymouth Breakwater or more relaxing up river trips to admire the beautiful scenery of both the Tamar and Lynher rivers. *Vyaj* was laid up for the Winter again in Coombe Creek and there was mercifully little work to do, as my stomach ulcer problem was now worse than ever. On a more positive note, two changes made our boating activities more convenient. My parents decided to buy a waterfront cottage only a stone's throw from our house at Saltash Passage. My father was nearing retirement and like me, his interests centred on the river so it made sense to live beside it instead of half a mile away up the steep hills of Saltash. Just across the road from their garden gate there were a string of beach moorings administered by the Ministry of Defence, so 'Pop' as he was affectionately known, could keep a dinghy there, put his cabin cruiser on a deepwater mooring close by and store his gear and do repair work in the little shed in the yard beside the cottage. He was only too happy to store gear for *Vyaj* and in many ways provided a more convenient base for our boating activities than the boathouse at Saltash because the Tamar Bridge was being built at this time and when it opened the steam ferry ceased to run. We had enjoyed the privilege of using the ferry for free, so close to our home, which landed on the Saltash side alongside our boathouse. The new Tamar Bridge was a blessing for people using road transport as it ended hours of queuing for the old ferry, but it cut the link between Saltash and Saltash Passage irretrievably on the day it opened. The same hand of fate that guided my parents to cross the river to live also guided us to move our mooring for *Vyaj* from the Saltash side of the river to a mooring space allocated to the Tamar River Sailing Club which now had premises on the old quay just down river from the ferry. As I had been a member since my teens and the club was now flourishing with Enterprise and then Albacore racing dinghies, some of the committee members encouraged us to put a deepwater mooring down close to the club, with the cunning idea that other cruising yachtsmen might follow our example and expand the club's membership and facilities. We could keep our dinghy on the club's storage space and we could operate from the Devon side of the river, still keeping the boathouse at Saltash for Winter storage of masts, dinghies and mooring equipment.

While cleaning and repainting our sixty odd blocks of iron ballast in March, one of our fellow club members put into my head the germ of an idea for replacing it economically with lead. "Melt it yourself" was the principle and some other club members in the building trade were asked to sell me any lead they came across instead of taking it to the scrap merchants. I acquired from my father in law an old washing boiler of the type that Victorian housewives used to heat over a coal fire to do the weekly wash. This was supported over a pit at the bottom of our garden on a couple of bits of old bed iron and logs and driftwood from the river provided free fuel. The kitchen was raided for a few cake tins, which were lined with 'plumbers black' (a crude graphite paste) to stop the lead sticking to the tins and when Peggy wasn't there to stop me I 'borrowed' her soup ladle to pour the molten lead to produce blocks the size of a brick, but with sloping sides which helped to wedge them in position. Six blocks weighed a hundredweight and by fitting out time I became the proud owner of 7 hundredweight of superb lead ballast at the cost of just under £9. This new ballast was considerably more efficient than the old cast iron and, more importantly, it was maintenance free and deposited no rusty sludge in *Vyaj's* bilge.

We floated *Vyaj* out of the creek in early April in preparation for the 1961 season. This followed the pattern of the previous seasons, with day trips, weekends at Newton Ferrers and the routine cruise in August battling against the rain, gales and fog of the British monsoon. After one particularly violent gale on the 3rd and 4th August while we were at anchor in 'The Bag' at Salcombe, we were struggling to start our Seagull outboard on the dinghy.

which had received a good soaking overnight and we needed its services fairly urgently to take us down river to Salcombe town, because my ulcer trouble was more than usually rampant and we needed milk and other bland foods to try to keep it under control. As expected with the rain still pouring down, the outboard would not start, so we began the usual routine of lifting it into the cockpit to the dry conditions under the cockpit cover, where we could clean and dry the plug and leads before trying again (using the right swear words) to get it to start. A friendly voice came from a 9 ton Gauntlet anchored nearby, offering us the use of his 14ft motor dinghy which he had hired from the town. We were already impressed by the very desirable cruising yacht and very pleasantly surprised that its owner would be kind enough to offer such down market yachtsmen as ourselves the use of his dinghy. When our outboard started we went over to express our thanks and we were promptly invited to come aboard for a drink in the evening.

We did not know that this visit was to be the start of a great friendship with the Abell family (Charles was the Chief Engineer of British Airways) and later his yachting partner Harry Hughes, who came to live opposite us on the Saltash side of the river. In spite of the bland food we brought back from Salcombe, my ulcer gave me no respite and much as I wanted to see this super yacht nearby, I was embarrassed by the fact that my ulcer diet forbade the consumption of alcohol. After being welcomed on board I threw caution to the winds and accepted a whisky and water from our host rather than cause any embarrassment by asking for a glass of milk instead. In the company of Charles, his wife Berry and teenage son John we soon relaxed and were chatting away like old friends while Charles kept generously topping up my glass. When we returned on board much later in the evening all my stomach pain had gone, and after the best night's sleep I had for weeks, I had some lasting improvement for the rest of the holiday thanks to the efficiency of Charles' medical prescription.

We also met Fiona Beal who was sailing her 6 ton gaff yawl *Devon Maid* to Cornwall and we have enjoyed a long friendship with her, after she settled in Port Navas and devoted herself to sailing, rowing, boatbuilding and woodcarving there.

On Monday August 7th we went up river to Kingsbridge in our dinghy in company with our new friends and then for lunch at the Crabshell Inn. In the evening we invited everyone on board *Vyaj*, (7 people and 1 dog) and our cosy cabin coped with entertaining them all, but we could see the barometer dropping rapidly and when they left at about 10:30 in heavy rain, another gale was already under way.

The gale proved to be a severe one and our friends from *Devon Maid* dragged their anchor and the next day's news broadcasts started with the accounts of 9 lifeboat callouts for yachts in distress on the south coast and damaged campsites, one which had been blown out to sea. As we waited several more days for the rain to stop, without success, we decided to sail back to Newton Ferrers anyway and the further we sailed, the heavier it rained and after anchoring in the Yealm at 15:00 we had to endure a continuous downpour all the evening and half the night. *Vyaj* had a completely unsheltered open cockpit where the helmsman (or woman) had to sit with a hand on the tiller and endure the cold and the rain that eventually leaked in through any oilskin. How we longed for a boat like *Bardu* with the sheltered "doghouse" and standing headroom down below.

We later went down channel for the second week of our holiday, revisiting our old haunts at St Mawes, Flushing and Helford. We then sailed home again via Fowey and our traditional last night anchorage at Newton Ferrers. After the usual day trips and weekend trips for the rest of the season, *Vyaj* was laid up again in Coombe Creek and as she had suffered some gale damage at the mooring we decided to give the topsides a complete burn off and repaint for the coming season.

We still had our boathouse at Saltash for storing the mast, boom, rigging and other gear, but it was an inconvenience to have to cross the river by dinghy to get to both the boathouse and the beach in Coombe Creek where *Vyaj* was laid up. When we were sitting on board *Vyaj* on her club mooring, I used to daydream about laying her up on the Plymouth side of the river where we lived, but the only suitable bit of beach we could see was private property, owned by one of our fellow club members who lived just down river from the club quay. Dreams of keeping our boat somewhere like that had to be put away like dreams of owning a boat twice the size of *Vyaj*. We had no idea that both dreams were to be realized in the next few years.

Looking back over our August fortnight holidays so far, they seemed to produce the same mixture: 3 fine days, 3 days of gales with heavy rain; 6 days of showery windy or cloudy weather, of a generally unpleasant character and the remaining 2 days composed of fog, flat calm or thunderstorms. But we always hoped that just one more Summer would provide the perfect weather we dreamed of.

Burning off the topsides paintwork began in February and the white boot topping was raised and altered in shape to improve its appearance and also to stop weed growing on it. The old galvanised iron 'horse' to which the mainsail was sheeted was going rusty so we replaced this with a phosphor bronze one made specially for us by Fox and Haggart. They also supplied bolts in the same material for the 'legs'. We replaced all the rope sheets and halliards with terylene, which was much more comfortable to handle and we bought a new 'pulpit' to fit around the foredeck.

We were ready for sea well before the Whitsun holiday weekend, which we spent sailing to Salcombe and back. Our Summer cruise took us back to Salcombe and then up channel for a change to Dartmouth and Dittisham. We remained at anchor there for a few days falling in love with the beautiful village and the upper reaches of the river above it. We sat out the inevitable 1st August gale there, before returning to Salcombe and then Newton Ferrers where we sat out the next gale and the miserable weather which followed. We returned home on a sunny August 12th. As usual the worst thing about the cruise was the weather and the best thing was meeting many friends, some old and some new, putting up cheerfully with the conditions.

It was rather depressing, however, to think that my teaching job would restrict us to an endless succession of cruises doomed to start in August and I could see no way of breaking this pattern,

Next year we fitted *Vyaj* out by early April and by way of an enjoyable change we used part of our Easter holiday to do a car tour of the Brittany coast with some friends. We came back home charmed by the Brittany coast and impressed by the dangers of all the outlying rocks. No good trying to visit it by sea in our restricted time in *Vyaj*. Nor was there much chance of spending much time in our beloved Isles of Scilly either. In a somewhat dejected frame of mind I was browsing through the pages of the Western Morning News a few days after our holiday ended, actually on Monday April 22nd 1963, when a small advertisement in the boats for sale section caught my attention, which read as follows:

"For Sale

13 ton Diesel Motor Yacht. New main BMC Commodore Diesel, hydraulic drive just delivered; wiring; 7Hp Kelvin TVO reconditioned 1963; extensive inventory, worth £2000; hull storm damaged; range 600 miles; offers around £800."

The hand of fate, guiding us towards the "Fortunate Islands" demanded investigation of this unusual advert. The fact that tonnage was given rather than measurements suggested a sturdy type of vessel. The low asking price hopefully could be explained by storm damage (which we could repair), the "new engine" and extensive inventory suggested that she had been well maintained before her unfortunate damage and that she had not come on the market cheaply as a result of old age, neglect or rot. My imagination saw the wake churning away behind a 60Hp diesel pushing 13 tons of dreamship down channel against adverse conditions a lot more impressively than 8Hp of Stuart Turner pushing a mere 4 tons and a half. It had to be investigated.

My suggestion to the family that we should go to Topsham to have a look at this wreck fifty miles away was greeted at first with laughter and incredulity. I wrote to the advertiser anyway asking permission to view her next weekend and the fact that most of my crazy ideas seemed to have worked out in the past produced a certain amount of cautious interest in the family.

The reply to my request to view *Fairwater* enclosed a detailed list of fittings and equipment. The list, to my humble eyes, seemed to have come from Aladdin's Cave: New mattresses and cabin seat backs; Echo Sounder; 180 ft. of calibrated 3/8 anchor chain (to fit the Moyle winch on deck) and a new 35lb. CQR anchor (*Vyaj's* 15lb. CQR had held us in all weathers). Fresh water tank of 80 gallons compared with our existing 4 gallons, electric bilge pump (new technology then), 1½ tons of iron ballast, searchlight, electric horn, navigation lights, boathooks, boarding ladder, helmsman's seat: a quick estimate of the purchase price of these items (most bought last year) added up to more than the asking price for the hull and engines.

Selling *Vyaj* would cover the cost of the damaged hull and extensive inventory, but could not meet the extra £400 asked for the new BMC Diesel. The answer was to make a reduced offer for the hull and equipment but no main engine and then start to worry about how we could get this wreck and her gear to Plymouth.

The weekend came and we drove to Topsham for a Saturday family outing, to meet the owner on Topsham Quay who would then guide us to Bickford's Yard out on the Exmouth road to look around. The owner pointed her out to us and the pile of salvaged equipment on the quay and tactfully disappeared.

Fairwater was lying on her side at a steep angle on the mud beside the river bank. We climbed on board with difficulty by a precarious ladder, to find that moving about the boat was difficult because the floor boards of the cockpit and the cabin were all thrown ashore and only the sloping bearers remained, made slippery with oil and mud. The cabin area was inches deep in oily mud with a foot or two of water in the port bilge. The starboard bunk was falling apart and the port bunk was missing. Daylight showed through some planks on the starboard bow. The whole interior looked, with good reason, as if it had been submerged in muddy, oily water. She looked and smelt, a complete wreck.

Painstakingly and awkwardly, in spite of the mess and the crazy angle, we checked all that we could of every rib, floor and plank in the bottom of the boat. We failed to find anything broken or rotten. The decking looked sound, except for two small patches over the after end of the cabin. From the outside the damage to the bow could be easily seen. The stem was shattered and partly missing, but the apron behind it was intact and the plank endings were all undamaged and securely fastened. Over the worst damage to the bow a lead patch had been fixed by the salvors to keep the water out during her tow from Topsham quay where she had swamped and sunk to the yard up river where she was lying.

Although the engines were out, the rudder, propellers and shafts were all undamaged, as was her handsome cruiser stern (pointed for seaworthiness as in most fishing boats) and even the delicate water cooling pipes for the diesel engine were intact. The wheelhouse, skylight and main deck covering were in a good state. Her shape was workmanlike and pleasing, her generous beam and headroom impressed us and she looked like a little ship rather than a rich man's plaything.

My mother was close to tears, not because of the problems and work ahead, but with sadness that such a basically beautiful specimen of the boatbuilder's art should have come to this shabby, neglected and forlorn end. It was decided that it was worth some negotiation to buy her cheaply and my parents offered to cover the purchase price until such time as we could sell *Vyaj* to cover the cost. As it happened, they never wanted to be refunded.

I wrote to the owner and offered £350 for the hull, equipment and Kelvin wing engine as against the £400 he was asking for the same plus the old Thorneycroft main engine. During the week he thought over the offer and finally wrote to accept it, saying that although our bid was not the highest, we were able to offer ready cash (thanks to my parent's help).

By May 3rd our deposit had been paid and we borrowed a van to collect some of the gear and at the same time to clear her out as far as possible. We watched her lift on the rising tide and only saw a steady trickle along either side of the keel, with no major leak from the damaged bow. The previous owner gave us a photo of *Fairwater* as she had been with a smart white hull with varnished teak wheelhouse, skylight and trim. Hopes were rising, but the great problem ahead was how to get *Fairwater* to the beach at Saltash Passage where work on her rebuild could go ahead.

Next weekend we made another visit to the owner at Topsham to hand over the rest of the purchase price and collect a few pieces of equipment from the yard of his house. He suggested to us, in all sincerity, that it would pay us to buy the new Commodore diesel, for which he was asking £350 and which with less than 100 hours of running, had now been stripped down, inspected by an insurance engineer and fitted with new electrical equipment. It was now literally as good as new. Moreover, all the controls and instruments were still in place and the engine bearers were all aligned and intact ready for that particular engine to be dropped back in again.

I could begin to see the logic of this idea, though we had no spare cash to finance it. Anyway, I said, I had seen adverts in the yachting magazines for

BMC Commodores for less than £450, so as he was asking £350 for a second hand one, was he prepared to drop his asking price?

He pointed out that by the time the engine, with hydraulic gearbox arrived it was over £500, regardless of what the magazine or adverts said. In addition he could show us bills for installation, changes and controls which brought his actual outlay to £830. Now we began to see that this virtually new engine for £350 was a bargain and would be a much simpler installation job than buying and fitting something different at some time in the future.

We promised to think this over and after a phone call to Sleeman and Hawking, the engineers at Teignmouth, who had worked on the engine to confirm what we had been told, we decided to try to raise the money from our bank. Peggy persuaded a rather reluctant bank manager to provide a loan, so yet another problem was solved but the biggest problem, bringing the boat home remained unsolved.

Were we to bring her by sea or by land? It would obviously be safer to bring a storm damaged boat by land, as the extent of the damage and subsequent leakage could not be accurately predicted. We found that to do this we had to (1) arrange a tow up river to Exeter to lift her out (2) arrange for a crane and a road transporter to be there at the right time (3) arrange a Police escort because of *Fairwater's* beam of over 11 ft. (4) ensure that the craning out and support on the transport would be done with great care, bearing in mind that the hull was already weakened and damaged (5) arrange another crane to be at the right place at the right time to off load and (6) put the boat in the right spot so that she could be left until tide and weather were correct for moving her to a beach mooring at Saltash Passage (7) find the money to pay for this and any extra expense that would be inevitable if the timetable did not run smoothly.

The alternative was potentially easier, but much more risky, i.e. to have her towed down the river Exe to the sea, then along the coast, past Start Point and Bolt Head, across Bigbury Bay and then across Plymouth Sound and finally up river to Saltash Passage. There a beach mooring could be laid right outside my parents cottage at the Riverside. The only civilian towage firm I could find at Plymouth didn't want to touch the job. But we did find a man who could! Fate led us to the Beach Hotel at Exmouth to Tom Lytton who was then Cox'n of the Exmouth lifeboat. He ran a pleasure boat business in the Summer. Over a couple of pints he agreed to do the job for £50, subject to inspecting the boat (which he already knew) and consulting Bickford's who had towed her to their yard and he agreed to do it as I requested, before the Whitsun bank holiday.

The other condition was that we would be responsible for arranging insurance for this escapade and accepted the salvage principle for payment:

No cure, No pay. If he delivered he got the money, if she sank he took no financial responsibility. How lucky that Peggy worked in the marine department of her Insurance office in Plymouth!

Fairwater had begun her lucky streak by finding the right person to see to her needs at the right time. Tom Lytton phoned on the evening of the 25th May to say that he was towing *Fairwater* down overnight. He knew from experience that overnight the sea tends to be calm. He had arranged for a fellow boatman to provide another passenger launch for the tow should there be difficulties off Start Point. He would keep a searchlight on *Fairwater's* white waterline and when he couldn't see it any longer he would know she was in trouble. If they successfully passed Start Point, he would anchor in Salcombe to wait for favourable tides to go on to Plymouth and his other boatman could return to Exmouth and he assured me he would put on board *Fairwater* if it were needed, the most efficient bilge pump in the world: "a frightened man with a bucket".

Next day I scrounged a lift from my school during the lunch hour to come down to the river's edge, to see *Fairwater* riding safely on a temporary deep water mooring, and my father told me he had seen to the mooring operation and sent Tom Lytton on his way back to Exmouth before lunchtime with the £50 in cash he had so thoroughly earned. To put this figure into perspective, it was as much as I earned for a fortnight's teaching.

To come into the mooring to sit safely on the beach, *Fairwater* needed a pair of bolt on legs to keep her upright. Her original pair had been shattered in the storm at Topsham, but the remains of one of them had been amongst the gear we had put on the lorry at Bickford's yard. Although beyond repair, it provided a pattern for a pair of temporary pine legs, with iron bolts, which my father made in his little workshop. Now *Fairwater* enjoyed the advantages of a berth just the other side of the road from my father's cottage. She also cast her spell in her artful way over my father who became a devoted admirer. His workshop stored her paints and brushes and he was easily persuaded to put his joinery skills into making a pair of fo'c'sle bunks in mahogany, with gleaming bunkboards, beautifully dovetailed drawers and storage cupboards underneath. I bought the mahogany, laid down the specifications and shamelessly allowed him to do the work as a labour of love. This furniture remains to this day, useful, beautiful and reassuring as the warm mahogany colours reflect the light when sunbeams shine through the portholes, or when the reading lights over the bunks glow on dark evenings. My specifications also demanded a chain shute for the anchor chain, a sail bin with a hinged lid and new teak floorboards, to transform what had been basic storage space into something like a yacht's fo'c'sle. Unhurriedly and meticulously, my father did it all.

Not that I stood back and let other people do all the work! The whole boat was stripped of all fittings and the few bits of furniture which survived the sinking. The whole interior was washed down with hot water and caustic soda so that every detail could be safely inspected, free of mud and oil. She began to smell like a boat, not a wreck. Next, in search of other possible problems, all the paint was burned off the topsides, a mass of dark blue paint with a mean little white waterline that did nothing to show off her beautiful shape. The new colour scheme was easy to decide. She had to wear the pale blue and white livery of her predecessor; anyway some tins of surplus paint were at hand for the purpose.

This detailed examination of the hull revealed only one area needing attention. A lead patch on the port side just aft of the leg position revealed some soft planking. A shipwright friend came down for a few evenings to scarf in 3 lengths of new planking to cure this problem in a craftsmanlike manner. This work had to be done between tides while we still enjoyed trips in *Vyaj*. So the Summer drew on until August when I decided to use my school holiday to put *Fairwater* at the top of the disused ferry beach on a Spring tide, so that I could work on her underwater area without interruption over a period of time when the tides were neaps.

The bottom was scraped, undercoated and antifouled. Extra fastenings were driven up into the oak floors and a new oak floor was fitted to replace one that had cracked. A split was found running along the lovely straight grain of the starboard garboard plank. The timber was pitch pine and as hard as iron, but the timber is subject to occasional splitting along the grain so there was no point in attempting the very difficult job of replacing it when copper 'tingle' could be fixed over the split to prevent any leakage when under way. The damaged stem was another job we thought ought to be tackled professionally and our local shipwright, Jimmy Donne supplied and fitted it and strengthened the bow, finishing it with a new bronze stemband and stemhead fitting, which would take the forestays of the ketch sailing rig with which I planned to replace the one small useless mast she carried when I bought her.

My amateur interest in boat design had convinced me that although *Fairwater* was designed as a motor yacht, she had the long heavy keel, broad beam with flat floor sections and large rudder that would enable her to sail quite well with favourable winds. There was no way she was designed as a primarily sailing hull, so there was no way she would sail up to windward. But who wants to struggle and tack against adverse winds when two engines sat under the wheelhouse floor ready and willing to push her speedily where we wanted her to go? Great is the satisfaction of the sailing purist who makes use of whatever winds may blow, but great also is the satisfaction of the motor sailor who has found his anchorage, dined in style on board and gone ashore for a pint while the purist struggles in after dark!

Which brings me to the point where I must sing the praises of the real hero of this story, the boat designer and builder called Percy Mitchell, who conceived and produced my beautiful *Fairwater* back in 1930. Coincidentally 1930 is the same year I was launched into the world myself. Percy will need no introduction to anyone with an interest in classic wooden boats. He was a man of giant strength and skill who set up his own boatbuilding firm after serving his apprenticeship in the charming little cove of Portmellon, next door to Mevagissey. He could only afford a net shed, the wrong side of the road from the sea to do his boatbuilding, but he had the confidence to cope with any problem that came along and his confidence was not misplaced. He built fishing boats of typical local design; he built a 72 ft. passenger vessel for Torquay; he built passenger launches for Charlie Cload at Plymouth and he built *Fairwater* before his reputation for first class craftmanship resulted in building the best of prewar yachts for wealthy owners to the designs of fashionable naval architects. He also built local working craft. Today, 65 years on, I count myself lucky to have owned and preserved one of his unique beautiful craft.

Fairwater was designed on the kitchen table of his cottage after hard days of work in the yard, as his widow remembered when I took *Fairwater* back to Portmellon a few years ago. I cannot trace *Fairwater's* original owner, but he must have asked for a fast, seaworthy launch, so Percy designed him a beamy double ended vessel with a traditional fishing boat shape, but built to a much lighter specification than a fishing boat to give her lift and speed. She was built on 'close seamed' construction principles using lightweight planking copper fastened to steamed oak ribs. 'Close seamed' means that narrow planks are so perfectly fitted that no space for caulking is allowed and every plank over its full length fits its neighbours so exactly that only a lick of paint is put between them. Over every curve and bend, there is no room for a millimetre of error. The timber, if light, was not flimsy. Pitch pine on the bottom, Norwegian spruce on the topsides, teak for the topstrake and exterior trim. Practically all of it is there today and is 'as sound as a bell'. Because of her construction, without the heavy sawn oak frames that one might expect, she has been able to bounce back from her misadventures. Like the trees she was built from, she could bend, and therefore would not break!

I only appreciated my luck in finding a boat with this pedigree as time went by, but after Percy retired and before he died shortly afterwards, I was able to correspond with him, after following his career in his book "*A Boat Builder's Story*". This personal link, though sadly short, is treasured. When beset by the problems, fatigue and setbacks of the *Fairwater* rebuild, I only had to think of Percy, his workload and his determination to tackle problems and overcome them, to draw on his strength of purpose and get on cheerfully with the work in hand.

While on the ferry slip, a local transport contractor, Stoneman's, brought the Commodore diesel down by lorry from Teignmouth and supplied a mobile crane to lift it in. Engine case, cockpit floorboards, cabin furniture, a new galley, a new toilet compartment, new wiring and light fittings filled all the available working hours. My cousin Roy Sanders did most of the electrical and mechanical work. We ordered a 12'6" Penguin sailing dinghy kit to build during the Winter as a new tender.

Looking back on this workload, after stressful days of teaching, it is not surprising that in November I was overtaken by rampant stomach ulcer problems and by January I found myself in hospital facing major surgery as nothing else could provide a cure. The operation was successful, but the months of diet before and the need to treat the patched up stomach and duodenum with care afterwards left me feeling fragile for several weeks. Then on the 4th week after the operation I started on the Penguin dinghy kit in the ground floor cellar at home. The early stages, making plywood panels, required little physical effort and provided an incentive to get back to fitness for the labours of the coming boating season. I was back to work at school in half the time estimated for convalescence, being rightly advised by my surgeon that the quickest way back to fitness was to fight rather than rest. I began weekend work sessions back on *Fairwater* in March and over the Easter holiday the main cabin was redesigned and rebuilt. The old cabin had a vast floor space, 6 feet wide, with two simple bench seats fitted with mattresses to use as bunks. This floor area was a waste of space and had no handholds if one were thrown across it in rough conditions at sea. I decided that a 3 feet floor space, with teak floor boards and a cabin table, two seat berths with pilot berths behind and deep storage cupboards beneath would be a great improvement. The cabin length, 8'6" would leave space aft of the bunks for 2' of hanging wardrobe one side and a navigation table with radio etc. the other. The old pine floorboards made the bunk tops which would not be seen under the mattresses and the finish was the same mahogany finish that had warmed our hearts on *Vyaj*, but now gave us space and headroom on a much grander scale. A new galvanised iron pulpit was purchased from Simpson Laurence for the bow, the original lifelines and stanchions altered to suit it and a coat of cream "Deckaflex" plastic was laid over the existing deck covering to smarten it up and provide extra waterproofing. Eight electric lights were fixed and the galley was stocked with cutlery, melamine crockery and cooking utensils, with an electric fan/ventilator overhead to deal with the steam.

On Saturday May 9th the Penguin was launched and given very satisfactory trials under sail, outboard and paddles. All that was now needed for *Fairwater* to put to sea within 12 months of her arrival was a good engineer to deal with the engine installation and again one appeared in the jovial form of Ben Shikovsky who agreed to devote as much spare time work as was necessary to get us mobile. The first engine trial was May 24th with the Kelvin 6/7 Hp paraffin auxiliary engine which took us off the mooring and up river at 3 to 4 knots, but proved almost impossible for manoeuvring because of its wing propeller installation with no rudder behind it.

A week's half term holiday at the end of May was used to put finishing touches to equipment and paintwork and the 14th June saw our first satisfactory run under diesel power. Now *Fairwater* came to life as the powerful diesel exhaust note roared away, responding to gear and throttle changes and effortlessly sped us along at 7 or 8 knots. This was a whole new world of sensation for us, used to pushing along at half that speed in *Vyaj* and now, instead of steering by tiller in an exposed open cockpit we had the shelter of a wheelhouse with generous headroom and complete shelter.

It did not take long to adjust to handling a larger and faster vessel and next weekend I had the confidence to take her into Sutton harbour to fuel up alongside Cload's pontoon. After a couple more day trips to Cawsand, with some mackereling off Penlee Point, the vibration of the new engine installation opened up several small leaks, which over a few days rose high enough to enter the gear box housing and then flooded the starting motor. The salt water had to be cleaned from this and the starter dried in the oven ashore before we could bring *Fairwater* back to the beach where three or four loose fastenings through the hull into the engine bearers were found, driven home and stopped to cure the leakage.

Ben came the following Thursday to replace the starter and check that all was well mechanically and we gave *Fairwater* her first sea trial the next weekend with cousin Roy and his wife June spending the first night afloat with us. We left the mooring at mid afternoon on Saturday, 3rd July, had an hour's fishing off the Mewstone and anchored in the Yealm in the Pool at Newton Ferrers mid evening.

Next morning we made an early start in fine sunny conditions, leaving at 07:10 and anchored in Salcombe harbour just after 10:00. We did some work on the electrics, enjoyed lunch in the sunshine in the cockpit and left again for home at 14:00. After pushing against the tide at gentle cruising revs we arrived safely back on the mooring at 18:00. *Fairwater* had taken us effortlessly in a day as far as we had got in our first fortnight's holiday in *Vyaj*.

The weekend after that we took my father with us and anchored for the night at Cargreen in wet and windy weather with a southwesterly gale forecast. We went down river to Cawsand for lunch then next day as the weather improved had tea off Jennycliff before returning by mid evening.

We had another weekend trip to Fowey and a number of family day trips during the rest of July and the first week of August, before deciding to risk our planned Summer holiday cruise starting August 7th, with Roy and June coming along to keep us company. We had doubts about how far we should go with *Fairwater* still incomplete and not thoroughly tested. Looking back I can see that the doubts were well justified. The best months for cruising, June and July had passed. We were having frequent teething problems with hull and engines. On the other hand we had those first essentials: a good anchor, a vast length of new anchor chain and a good anchor winch. We had years of small boat handling experience. We had three weekend trips and half a dozen day trips under our belt and had not yet come to grief. We had a good compass, a Walker trailing log (both ex Admiralty) sufficient charts and a radio to check on the weather forecasts. The Scillies beckoned and the spirit of Percy Mitchell said "Get on with it and tackle the problems as they come". We had our new Penguin dinghy astern with her Seagull outboard safely stored on board and her sailing gear wisely left at home. We had been this way before in *Vyaj*. This was just a new 'venture' for yet one more Summer.

As might be expected, unfriendly southwesterly's with grey skies were blowing when we picked up Roy and June from the pier at Saltash on Friday evening, August 7th. It was too late to face headwinds and darkness down channel so we ran around the Mewstone to anchor in the Yealm for the night.

The next day, after shopping in Newton Ferrers we decided to press on against the contrary southwesterly's to Fowey, leaving at 14:30. It took five hours of dreary slog in wind and rain to reach Fowey, while Roy and June battled with sea sickness, until we ran up river from Fowey harbour to anchor in the peace and quiet of Wiseman's Pool, where a good evening meal was appreciated by all on board.

The next day proved the value of our Penguin tender. We used it to go down river, past the china clay loading quays and through Fowey harbour to Polruan in the afternoon and in the quiet of the evening we went up river on the top of a Spring tide through the tree lined creek that leads to Lerryn.

After a day of rest in the Helford river, we tentatively headed for the Lizard at 07:30 to check if conditions were right to press on to Scilly. All was well, except for heat haze and June's sea sickness. We crossed Mount's

Fairwater as we first saw her, storm damaged at Topsham on the river Exe.

Fairwater, repainted on the slip at Saltash Passage after being towed from Exmouth to Plymouth.

With Ian Sutherland Jones, the surgeon who gave me a life saving operation.

The beautiful harbour of St. Mary's, in the Isles of Scilly.

Fairwater as rebuilt, off St. Mary's harbour, towing the 'Fairey' dinghy which performed so well.

With Joan Leach in Fairwater's cosy cabin.

Gutting mackerel was all part of the skipper's duties.

Skip and Ike, as experienced crew, felt entitled to comfortable seating while being taken ashore.

The crew are admiring the scenery around Cromwell's Castle, Tresco Channel.

Nephew Andrew Davy, Harry Hughes and ourselves enjoy a visit to the 'Turk's Head', St.Agnes.

Havssula, Harry Hughes' boat anchors beside us in Porthcressa.

Rare arrival in flat calm: Crow Sound ahead.

The Birdman's cottage on Bryher for the film "When the whales came".

The Cornwall police band, whose excellent musicianship provoked howls and barks of protest from Skip.

Fairwater on the grid at the bottom of our garden for serious work on the hull
AND

after much effort, ready for sea again with gleaming paintwork.

Running down Channel to Scilly.

Passing the granite headland of Peninnis, St. Mary's.

Island activities: watching the gig racing

and 'shrimping' in cold weather.

Bant's Carn passage burial chamber.

Our great friends Alba and Roger come alongside.

Scilly ruins: one of the cottages on Samson.

The blockhouse at Old Grimsby, Tresco.

The site on Nornour which yielded the hoard of brooches and Roman coins.

The cairn on Great Ganilly marking the possible site of a primitive lighthouse.

Fairwater moored in the inner harbour, St. Mary's, for essential repairs to her rudder.

The last apple trees to be found in Tresco Abbey gardens, overlooking Appletree Bay, still interestingly associated with beehives: for cider and mead?

Our house (top right), workshop, boatstore and quay (at waterlevel) with Fairwater on her mooring.

The terrace of our house, which overlooks the river.

Scillonian events: the capsized crane.

Derek Pickup's birthday lunch. Betty Pickup on right.

Bay, past Mousehole with its memories of our trip in *Vyaj,* at 12:30 and followed the coast towards Land's End to take our departure from the Runnel Stone Buoy at 13:15. During what seemed to be an endless afternoon crossing the shipping lanes towards Scilly, with visibility still restricted by the haze, we came in well up to the north of our intended course, pushed that way by the northerly running tide with which we have subsequently become familiar.

As it was, with many ineffective attempts to get a D/F radio bearing on Round Island we found ourselves between St Martin's and Round Island and had to work our way against the tide past the Eastern Islands and St Mary's, before we could round Peninnis Head and come to anchor in St Mary's harbour. After hours of anxiety we had arrived through waters that were later to become as familiar as the proverbial back of one's hand.

As we arrived RMS *Scillonian II* was backing away from the quay and we anchored quickly inshore to take the dinghy in to buy provisions before the shops closed. A good night's sleep followed by some fine warm weather put us in the mood for an exploration of the Islands in the dinghy so we headed for Tresco Channel. We found our way past the Hulman to New Grimsby and walked to Cromwell's Castle and returned to Appletree Beach, where we lunched, lying in the sun and enjoying the scenery from this half mile stretch of almost white sand, undisturbed by the other five people who shared with us the good fortune to be in these idyllic conditions. We found our way back to *Fairwater* about teatime and in the evening found a memorable meal at the 'Bar Escapade', then a lovingly run small restaurant, but now, inevitably, holiday flats, which put the finishing touches to a very satisfactory day.

The next day, Friday, we had to come back to reality and the need to get Roy and June back within reach of home by Sunday, when their holiday ended. We decided to head back while the going was still good. We left St Mary's at 06:45 and ran into one of our inevitable teething problems about half an hour later, just as we were being thrown about in the choppy seas caused by the 'Menawethan Race'. On the instrument panel the needle of the ammeter was showing some erratic behaviour and on lifting the lid of the engine box the problem was only too apparent. The bolts securing the dynamo had vibrated loose and dropped into the bilge. Unfortunately the drive belt also drove the cooling water supply pump to the diesel exhaust hose and silencer and if we didn't want a fire in the bilge we had to reinstate the whole system. The engine case had to be dismantled, the nuts and bolts retrieved from the bilge and appropriate spanners found to reinstate the whole system while *Fairwater* continued to wallow in the short steep seas. Roy and Peggy between them performed this service, going slightly green in the process, while I, as skipper, kept a lookout on the distant horizon. Once more underway we made the seemingly endless passage past Land's End, happy to find the Runnel Stone Buoy at 11:20, then rounding Lizard at 14:00 and heading for Helford, only faced with one more delay. Off Coverack there was a group of small fishing boats busy handlining for mackerel. Speed had to be reduced and our lines put out to catch that most delicious of all suppers: fresh fried mackerel. The delay was not long, we caught seven beauties in about 4 minutes (just the number we wanted) and then returned to normal cruising revs, dropping anchor off Helford Village at 17:00.

A run of ten hours which included a stop for engine repairs and a slow down for fishing was very satisfactory and only a little longer than our many runs in subsequent years.

Next morning (Saturday 15th August) we made a leisurely trip across Falmouth Bay from Helford, past Falmouth Docks and up to our familiar anchorage spot off Flushing. In the evening we went ashore at Falmouth to book Sunday lunch at the Greenbank Hotel. We were to be joined there by both my father and Peggy's father who were to drive down and then take Roy and June home to Saltash by road after lunch.

That evening after visiting some friends at Flushing we decided it would be prudent to leave this anchorage where we were close to other boats and amongst permanent moorings as gales were forecast. We went back to St Mawes and a little way up the Percueil River, not as full of moorings as now and dropped our anchor with the rising gale beginning to sing through the rigging and thankfully turned into our bunks for the night.

The gale lasted throughout the whole of Monday and Tuesday, making our daily excursions ashore in the dinghy quite exciting. The riverside road into St Mawes became autumnal with brown leaves and green pine needles ankle deep along the pavement. Summer cruising was over. While ashore on Tuesday we phoned a young friend from Plymouth, Tony Killock and invited him to join us on Wednesday for the run back to Plymouth.

He came by train to Falmouth, then via the St Mawes ferry in time to join us for a Ploughman's lunch in the "Rising Sun" at St Mawes. The gale had been replaced by sunny, blustery conditions and we spent the rest of the day visiting Falmouth for diesel fuel and watching the racing in the bay with everything from Sea Scorpions (raced by friends of ours from Plymouth) to the Falmouth work boats with their large gaff sails and large efficient crews. We had a run up river sightseeing to Mylor and Restronguet and returned to anchor for the night off St Mawes.

On Thursday August 20th we ran up channel, still delighting in our passage making ability, past Plymouth (via the Eddystone Light) and on to Salcombe for the night.

Friday was a rest day when we left *Fairwater* for the golden beaches opposite Salcombe Town, loading the Penguin with cushions, towels etcetera and lunching in the sunshine on crab salad, hock, fresh peaches and cream.

"Not a bad life if you don't mind roughing it" became one of our bywords on *Fairwater* for such treats as this. On Saturday we returned to the Yealm and Sunday after lunch at Cawsand in the lee of the inevitable southwesterly we ran back up river to pick up our mooring by 16:00. *Fairwater* had brought us safely home: she had shown us the delights of Fowey, Falmouth, Helford, Scilly, the Yealm and Salcombe and we had lived comfortably on board most of the time with guests to share the pleasure.

The work and the expense now seemed justified. Much more work had to be done. The abiding memory was the visit to Scilly, however brief and the longing to return there, for just one more Summer next year.

The season ended with a dozen or so day trips with assorted friends, perhaps the most rewarding one being when we took Ian Sutherland Jones and his family out for the day to Cawsand for lunch and then to the Yealm for tea; most rewarding because I could enjoy a pint ashore with Ian at Cawsand as he was the surgeon who had operated on my stomach so that I was able to enjoy such privileges.

Chapter Four

1965 to 1975

Fairwater spent most of the Autumn and Winter afloat on her mooring, receiving a visit every couple of weeks to run the diesel, charge the batteries and check that all was well generally. At home I worked on the hall, staircase and bathroom but the Christmas holiday saw me back on board to start the reconstruction of the cockpit which now looked crude and down at heel, compared with the new accommodation below. After stripping out the old woodwork, the narrow brown painted seats were replaced by wider ones made of varnished mahogany with tongue and grooved seatbacks to match. The cockpit floor bearers were strengthened and properly shaped floorboards were made, finished with iroko, left unvarnished to provide a non slip surface.

A major new floorbeam, about 4" x 5" thick and 11' long was put right across the after end of the engine case to take the tabernacle for the new mizzen mast and this conveniently linked up with a strong oak pillar off the keel which looked as if it might have been a support for a steering wheel when *Fairwater* was originally built without a wheelhouse. The new mizzen, 27' long was made of solid spruce, matching the larger hollow spruce main mast that Jimmy Donne made for us which we had carried stepped on the main deck last year, where it carried useful deck lights and navigation lights but as yet no sail. The mizzen was to be ready to carry sail for our projected Whitsun cruise and the Donnes supplied the blocks, mast fittings, boom and rigging; John McKillop of Kingsbridge made the brown sail.

The cockpit rebuild was so complicated and working time afloat so restricted that work was still proceeding when we came in to the beach off my parent's cottage for fitting out in early April. The complete repaint outside was aided by a week's dry and reasonably warm weather. Some details of improvement to the accommodation and engine case were also carried out and *Fairwater* was back on her mooring and ready for a day's trial run by the last day of my Easter holiday on Sunday April 30th. In the next few weeks we improved the installation of the Kelvin wing engine and after three more trial runs, including a night on board at Cargreen and a visit to Cload's pontoon for 55 gallons of diesel fuel and the completion of the mizzen we were ready to leave for a week's Whitsun cruise. For the first few days we took with us the Isbell family (Dick, Peter and Brian) all with salt water in their veins inherited from fishermen and boatbuilders of that name who lived for generations in Looe.

Friday June 4th 1965 came along and we had made it a point of honour that we would get to sea as soon as possible after work, so by 18:00 we were on our way down river, an hour later were off Rame Head and conditions were fair to go down channel, setting course for Fowey but hoping to go on to Falmouth if possible. By 21:15 we could see the leading light into Fowey and before darkness fell we took a good bearing on Dodman Head and so decided to press on. Unfortunately we had to deviate from our compass course in the dark to zigzag our way around a fleet of drift net fishing boats out after pilchards or herring, each lying to a mile or so of nets with lit Dan buoys to mark them. Thus we proceeded 'blind' and unsure of our course towards Falmouth helped only by the glow in the sky of the street lights at Falmouth which went out promptly at midnight.

St Anthony's Head light house eventually guided us in and we carefully picked our way towards St Mawes where we thankfully dropped our trusty anchor at 01:00.

After shopping at St Mawes next morning we left after lunch for the Helford river, catching enough mackerel to feed the crew and anchored again off Helford village at about tea time to stay for the night.

As Dick had to be back at work on Tuesday, we decided we must head back up channel while conditions were good so that he could be within easy reach of Plymouth on Monday. We left Helford in beautiful sunny conditions to enjoy going to sea through that enticing river entrance in the early morning light. Off Falmouth we found we were blessed with a following breeze over the starboard quarter so we hoisted the mizzen to let it do its first bit of real work and as we ran up the coast we took a tool kit up on deck and fastened the sheet leads for the jib, so that by the time we were off Looe we were able to switch off engines and gently move up channel under sail for the first time. As expected, Percy Mitchell's beautifully balanced hull allowed *Fairwater* to steer herself with only minimal help from the steering wheel and encouraged us to look forward to the future when we could organise the track, boom and halliards to fit her with her designed mainsail.

As we got nearer to Plymouth we held a crew conference to consider the possibility of going on to Salcombe where we could spend the bank holiday Monday and send Dick home by bus, so that his boys could enjoy an extra day on board before he brought his car up on Tuesday evening to take them and their gear back home to Plymouth.

Dick not only agreed to this very inconvenient programme but took home with him on the bus a couple of live crabs which he and the lads bought from a fishing boat *Bolt Head Lady* moored beside us, which he cooked, dressed and brought back with him next evening, so that we could all have a magnificent crab salad as main course for our farewell dinner.

The trip from Helford to Salcombe took less than eight hours and the log we streamed astern showed an easy cruising speed of seven and a quarter knots, which over the following decades, in spite of changes of engine power, still usually proved to be our average speed.

Returning home by the end of the week via Newton Ferrers for three days we decided not to cover too many miles at sea because we had detected two small but steady leaks that gave us some cause for concern. Water was leaking around the stern timbers where the main propeller shaft ran and an oil leak had developed around the tappet cover on the Commodore diesel engine that deposited a trickle of black oil down the engine and into the bilge all the time it was running. We enjoyed our stay in the Yealm, making friends with Cuth and Kate Harrison who were anchored there on their 72' 'Fleur de Lys' motor yacht *Vivione.* The propeller shaft coupling was also in need of frequent tightening, so we looked forward to putting *Fairwater* back on the beach to sort out these defects before our Summer holiday. It was a bit depressing having these little problems to sort out, especially after visiting *Vivione* which was so large, luxurious and new.

Most of our problems, we discovered in the following weeks, were all related to one hidden defect. To sort it all out, *Fairwater* again showed her ability to attract the right person to deal with it and established a long lasting friendship for ourselves. Our first engineer friend felt unable to commit himself to our requirements this year because of work and family responsibilities but he recommended a colleague who had the skill and enthusiasm to overcome any difficulty. So Ron Gray came on the scene.

"He's a bit of a character" said Ben, "Don't take any notice if he pulls your leg a bit." Ben was right about Ron who had a great sense of fun, shoulders like an ox, was a very fit Judo expert who relished any challenges and difficulties and who was particularly well equipped to deal with our diesel as he spent his working life as a senior engine tester in the diesel workshops in the Dockyard. His never ending store of funny stories, told with great verve and expertise cheered us up immensely as he doggedly chased the source of our problems. Shaft, propeller, couplings, engine casings were all stripped down and subjected to examination by micrometer and clock gauge; no bolt stud or keyway resisted his spanners and he never resorted to using a hammer, which he claimed was not an engineering tool at all. Thanks to his persistence the oil leak around the tappet cover was cured. The engine was realigned with an improved coupling and the prop shaft stern bearing was examined and replaced. But after everything was perfectly aligned Ron was still not happy with the vibration when under power. Out came the shaft and coupling and both went to a precision engineer who had the equipment to alter the keyways in the coupling, only to find that the shaft in the coupling had been installed off centre in the first place, so all efforts at lining up the coupling perfectly to the engine had been a waste of time. All was now put right and we could see the cause of the stern leak because the propeller shaft had increased the minute error over every foot of its length and had been whipping and jerking the stern timbers around the stern bearing, loosening their joints and so causing the leak.

Ron's financial rewards were few and later became non existent as he became a regular member of the crew together with his wife Vi and son Peter. We had several enjoyable weekend trips with various friends during the rest of July and went off for our fortnight's cruise, taking Roy and June with us for the first week, leaving Saltash at the first possible moment as usual at the end of work on Friday July 30th. Scilly was not on our minds as a destination this year for two reasons. Firstly we agreed to be back in the Plymouth area at the end of the first week to change crews, when Roy and June would be replaced with young Peter Isbell and our nephew Ian Davy. Secondly we were involved in selling our house on Normandy Hill in order to buy (we hoped) a dream house further down river.

We had lived in our old house for ten years and when not working on boats, Peggy and I had improved it and redecorated it the way we wanted. Peggy was very pleased with it, with its extensive river views (visitors said "It's like living in a lighthouse" because of its three storey site on a steep slope) and she felt she could live there for ever. I always dreamed, however, of a house with its own foreshore, where *Fairwater* could sit on the beach at the bottom of the garden and receive all the attention I wanted to lavish on her. From *Fairwater's* mooring off the Tamar River Sailing Club at Saltash Passage I often looked ashore at a sheltered beach overlooked by oak and beech trees beside the house owned by a couple of elderly club members and wondered if one could rent or buy it from them, as they showed no sign of using it for their dinghy sailing activities. Then early in 1965 the unexpected happened and they put the whole property on the market as they had reached retirement age and proposed to emigrate to New Zealand to live close to their only daughter. They were asking what was then a high price for the property (detached house with foreshore for £5,500!) on the very reasonable grounds that if they could not get their asking price they would not be able to afford to move to New Zealand and would happily stay where they were.

Peggy was not easily persuaded to view it but said she would go along with me if I made all the arrangements, hoping that that would be the last of the matter. Next Saturday, after lunch (traditional Cornish pasty made by my mother at her cottage) I announced to a surprised Peggy that arrangements had been made to view in a few minutes time, so we went the few hundred yards along the road from No. 900 to No. 863 Wolseley Road. The house faces the river, with spectacular views over its steeply sloping garden running down to the river's edge. It had privacy, charm, scope for extension and most important, a copse of mature trees beside it, sloping down to the sheltered beach, with a stone faced quay which, if cleared of debris, would be big enough for a workshop. We showed cautious interest but as we left we could both barely resist jumping for joy at having found the Ideal Home for our particular needs. We could put *Fairwater* on the beach for the Winter, use the workshop on the quay to maintain her, we could bring the mooring a few boat lengths down river and she would be sitting right outside our bedroom windows. So our house became another thread of the story, almost an accessory to *Fairwater*, enabling us to maintain and improve the boat so that our hopes of annual voyages to Scilly could become a reality.

We did not haggle over the price, but it took months of negotiation to sell our existing house and arrange a modest mortgage to cover the difference before the house became ours in September 1965.

For the next few years work on the house, garden and quay took precedence over cruising in *Fairwater*, other than Summer holiday trips to Falmouth and weekend and day trips closer to home.

Then in the late '60's *Fairwater's* deck began to leak with occasional drops on to the cabin bunks and soft patches appeared on the edges of the deck up for'd. I began to consider the possibilities of doing a complete redecking. I was forced to face the depressing choice of either disposing of *Fairwater* for what I might get for her (not much) or building a grid over our beach where she could be jacked up above high tide level for a major rebuild.

The grid was constructed on the beach, with great efforts put into moving large slabs of rock and laying concrete cross pieces, but we were still faced with jacking the hull up above high tide level and the removal of both engines, the wheelhouse and all the decking and deck beams. The necessary demolition and reconstruction was a daunting task for a part time impoverished amateur, with the certainty of spending vast amounts of effort and scarce finances, with no guarantee of a successful outcome.

A motley selection of second hand jacks was accumulated and a pile of wooden blocks and just when the whole project seemed to be getting too big and demanding, we went down river on the day after HMS *Scylla* was launched from the dockyard and *Fairwater* found a set of large beechwood wedges that had floated out with her and had probably not been worth retrieving by the Admiralty, as *Scylla* was the last warship planned to be built at Devonport dockyard. There were over a dozen of these wedges, each nearly 4 feet long and a foot wide and how they had not been found by the eagle eyed boatmen of Torpoint for twenty four hours I cannot imagine. I think that *Fairwater*, not for the first or the last time, had found the means of survival herself. The wedges were quietly retrieved without attracting the attention of the patrolling Admiralty Police launches and brought home. They proved to be an inspiration to the deck rebuild and were of use for many years to come when *Fairwater* needed to be jacked up on the grid again.

The long process of breaking up the old deck and removing the wheelhouse and all the other fittings went ahead slowly. *Fairwater* became an empty shell with all the deck beams removed except the one into the after end of the deck which was fortunately sound and chains were fitted through the portholes, tightened by rigging screws, to keep the hull in shape. Both engines were removed, with the big Commodore diesel being stowed at the back of our garage at home, taken from Saltash Town Quay where it was lifted out on Ron Gray's trailer and put on a rig for him to give it a thorough refit before being put back.

Before putting any deck beams back I realised that we had the opportunity to increase the headroom throughout by adding an extra plank to the hull, secured to new steamed oak timbers which could be extended downwards and copper riveted in beside the old ones to strengthen the whole topsides.

My cousin Roy now had a boat of his own, a Francis Jones designed Haven motor cruiser which had a similar deck line to my idea of *Fairwater's* new one and Roy's Haven had a foredeck one plank lower, that looked quite practical. Working the winch and the anchor was made easier by being not too high out of the water and if I used the same principle on *Fairwater* I could leave in the existing sound fo'c'sle beams and keep the winch and chain chute in their original positions over the new decking.

I was not worried about decreasing *Fairwater's* stability by the new raised piece of deck, which would only be nine or ten inches high anyway, because by removing the heavy oak framework around the skylight, now no longer needed to give headroom in the middle of the cabin and by replacing the thick pine deck planking with two layers of marine plywood I could decrease the weight of the deck enough to counterbalance its extra height. By laying each sheet of 'ply' in top quality glue over the joins in the layer beneath I would have a strong leakproof deck and by laminating new beams instead of cutting them out of larger sections of solid timber, I could save even more weight.

Getting the camber of the new deck right was a worry until I found that if I made an accurate jig, big enough and strong enough to laminate the largest beam, all the beams could be formed on it and simply cut to the required length by measurement from a common centre line. If the top plank of my new design was straight and all the new beams cut to exactly the same curve, the whole deck, when finally glued and fastened, would become very strong and easy to lay in big sheets. But how to get just the right curve? The simple answer lay in copying it from the one original beam still in position, which would ensure that the new deck would be built to the same curve as the old one.

I ordered the sawn oak battens for the laminated beams from the cheapest local sawmill, the whole project had to be done cheaply because it was running at the same time that we were spending money on adding a new sunroom to the house and building stone terrace walls in the garden. I just could not see how I could bolt together a strong jig over 12ft long on which the new beams could be glued and clamped into place, maintaining the curve accurately and evenly over the whole length. One morning, on going down to the quay, the answer was on the beach, lying beside *Fairwater's* bow, as a dog might proudly drop a retrieved stick. *Fairwater* had found a length of pitch pine fendering, about two feet square in the middle, eight or nine feet long and its top was cut into a curve, not very different from the curved template I had made for the beams. Curved fendering of this kind was put around the granite stonework of the dry dock entrances in the dockyard to save damage to ships being floated in. Cross pieces could be notched and screwed there securely, overhanging this baulk by a few inches, to which a few sets of 'G' clamps (already to hand) would pull the seven oak laminations into shape and hold the joints evenly under pressure while the glue set. The beams became a time consuming job because I had no planer/thicknesser in those days, so every piece had to be hand planed to an even and accurate thickness from the rough sawn oak. Over a hundred of these battens were needed, as each beam had seven laminates, each three eights of an inch thick.

Fourteen or fifteen beams were made this way, while the extra plank and ribs were bent into place and fastened and a year slipped by in the process, with the certainty that another year 'on the beach' would have to follow making a two and a half year timetable for the whole job. During the Summer we would often take a lunch time break at the weekend for a beer at the Royal Western Yacht Club which was on its old site at West Hoe then and we would sometimes lean on the sea wall, looking over Plymouth Sound, busy with boating activity and smell the salt tang of the sea breeze, wondering whether I was mad to get involved in all this work on such an old large boat.

Just when I might have bitterly resented the loss of two good Summers' boating the hand of fate opened another door leading on my obsession with Scilly. A very good friend of ours had business contacts with a bank manager n St Mary's. We had met Derek Pickup and his wife Betty when we visited hem on our first trip to Scilly in *Fairwater*. They were very kindly people ınd soon became our firm friends. Derek was keen on sailing and was also)bsessed with Scilly, refusing to let his bank move him away after a few /ears in the normal way. He took pity on our boatless condition and we were nvited to stay for a couple of weeks, becoming the first guests to stay at heir new cottage. Derek's day sailer *Suzanne* was ideal for shallow water :ruising around the Islands and he did me the invaluable service of showing ne around the main channels with their marks and transits. We zigzagged)ast the Hulman into Tresco Channel, finding our way between Bryher and Tresco by lining up Plumb Island with the little shop on New Grimsby Quay. We threaded our way between the Eastern Islands, sorting out the two Ganillys from the two Ganinicks, saying "hello" to the seals on Menawethan)efore heading towards the bare pyramid of Hanjague and then landing on Nornour to see the old bronze age hut circles there. We went around the back' of St Martin's and the 'back' of Bryher and we landed on Samson Bar intentionally!) We didn't visit St Agnes but the pilotage there from St Mary's s straightforward anyway.

Derek's overriding passion in life was catching prawns (always called shrimps' in Scilly) on the low Summer Spring tides and he showed me where to go and how to catch them but it was many years later that he revealed he closely guarded secrets of the very best places. Next to my father, Derek aught me more than anyone else of the delights of boating and my debt to him endured and widened as the years went by. In 1969 we went again and what I had forgotten from the first year was recalled, committed to memory and never forgotten. We were able to repay Derek a little for his undemanding kindness many years later as his health failed, but his love of the sea did not and we took him around the Isles in *Fairwater's* sheltered wheelhouse, 'ollowing the courses he had shown me so many years before.

The two seasons on the beach interrupted my routine keeping of a log of events, to which I frequently refer in the course of this story and facts and dates for a few years have completely disappeared from memory, as they will do unless written down, be it ever so briefly, at the time. But *Fairwater* was successfully rebuilt, the engines replaced, the facilities on board mproved, the wheelhouse almost doubled in size, the chart table moved to a new wheelhouse shelf where it was so easy to use and we were back to Summer cruises to Scilly in school Summer holiday time before the series of logs recommences with details from 1973.

At this stage another member of the devoted crew of admirers who worked for love, never for money, on *Fairwater* must be brought into the story. Back n the days of our ownership of *Vyaj*, when we frequently crossed the river to Saltash to the boathouse or the mooring, we always saw a polite, smiling little lad, usually in Wellington boots, either playing with model boats with one of his pals or just gazing with delight at the river and all that was going on there. Eventually he would guard our dinghy if we brought it to the beach for a short time, never presuming to get into it or play with it but he would hold it and look after it in the occasional wash from passing craft and you could tell from his attitude that nobody would dare touch this vessel while it was in his charge.

Peggy first suggested that Phil might enjoy being taken across the river in the dinghy and from there on, without ever pushing himself forward, he became a part of our boating activities and, as I can see it now, became hopelessly trapped into our obsession with our special boat and a very special group of islands. As I worked in the garden, Phil mixed cement and pushed wheelbarrows. When quay facilities were built or *Fairwater* came in on the grid Phil was always there. Always ready to help but never in the way. When Ron Gray was bewitched into the *Fairwater* group, Phil happily became hi Gopher... "You gopher this.....you gopher that." He watched Ron and learned and later became a workmate of his in the dockyard. It was Phil who held the 'dolly' as we rivetted the new top plank on to *Fairwater's* hull. It was Phil who was always on hand when engines were worked on or lifted ou and Phil who always was there to assist as our tumbledown bit of quay became a two storey boat store and workshop. Phil loved the occasional day trips but he stood happily by (and probably with a sense of relief) when *Fairwater* headed down river for a holiday cruise, or a venture towards the Isles of Scilly.

By August 1973 when we followed our usual urge to get to sea as soon as work finished on a Friday, we set out down river mid evening, with nephew Andrew and Richard Davy, both young schoolboys on board as crew. Phi was now an electrical fitter in the dockyard and was becoming increasingly useful to *Fairwater*, so he was probably more pleased than ever to see her on her way. We anchored at Cawsand for the night in ideal light north to northwest winds, settled the boys and the gear into the fo'c'sle and visited Dr. and Mrs. Bearblock, acquaintances from Saltash, on board their yacht *Penrosa* before the crew fell into their bunks and slept the deep and immediate sleep of the happily exhausted.

Next morning we were breakfasted and off down channel just befor 08:00. anchoring at St Mawes at 14:15, in spite of slowing down for a spell of fishing off Falmouth entrance. For an old lady, *Fairwater* certainly knew how to lift her skirts and run, to cover so much ground so quickly without being pushed. The afternoon saw much rowing, swimming and deck scrubbing performed by the young crew. Next morning we were off at 07:1

after hearing a good shipping forecast, rounding Lizard at 9:50, passing the Runnel Stone Buoy at 13:00 and after bribing our young crew with a packet of crisps for the first one to sight the Islands, we anchored at 17:00 in St Mary's harbour. To celebrate our arrival we dined at Tregarthen's Hotel with Peggy's father and our friends the Chritchlow family, who had all been infected by our Scillies Fever.

We then enjoyed eight blissful days in the Islands taking friends around with us, spending one night anchored in Tresco Channel and the rest in our favourite spot near the lifeboat slip in St Mary's. After one rest day in harbour after we arrived we were out around the Islands every day, catching fish, exploring islands and visiting as many different anchorages as possible.

When anchored alone in a tiny sandy cove on Little Arthur a crowded tripper boat passed by and the skipper shouted

"Seventy three coffees please!" A sketch map in the log shows *Fairwater's* tracks going around all the Islands except St Martin's. We were beginning to reap the benefits of all the work on *Fairwater*. She was proving to be a fast seaworthy home afloat, ideal for quick passages to Scilly and inter-island trips on arrival.

Our run back to the Mainland on Monday August 27th was beset by fog and drizzle. The forecast was for light winds and we left the Islands in reasonable visibility but as we approached Land's End at 09:00 it disappeared in the murk and we set a course to close with the land, hoping to see the Runnel Stone buoy and Tater-Du lighthouse to keep a check on our progress against contrary tide.

Visibility improved off Tater-Du Point fortunately and we set course across Mounts Bay, giving the Lizard a good clearance. As we approached the next landfall, we ran into heavy drizzle and poor visibility once again and decided to close in to identify the white buildings and lighthouse on the Lizard, rather than turn too soon into Falmouth Bay and find ourselves on the rocks in Kynance Cove. The Lizard was identified and safely rounded by 15:00. We could relax a little and slowed down for some mackerel fishing, using our old Kelvin wing engine to push us along at three knots. Ten fish provided excitement for the boys and a supper for all hands. Then back on diesel engine only, pushing on to St Mawes to anchor at 17:30.

Tuesday was a rest day at St Mawes, Wednesday was an early morning start for Fowey to avoid the rain forecast with a southwesterly four to five wind, which caught up with us after our arrival. Thursday was an afternoon run up channel to our beloved Pool anchorage in the Yealm, where we happily spent two more days and treated our crew to an end of voyage celebratory meal at the Old Ship Inn before returning home on Sunday.

The most interesting innovation for the 1974 season was the new suit of sails ordered from John McKillop at Kingsbridge. A working jib, a big genoa that set on the forestay to the masthead and a loose footed mainsail hoisted on an aluminium track on the mainmast now supplemented the existing mizzen, giving *Fairwater* a balanced rig with enough sail area to push her along in a moderate breeze, but not enough to overwhelm her if caught out in a real blow. Other improvements were an Avon inflatable dinghy which we stored on the wheelhouse roof in addition to the dinghy we towed astern. This could act as a life raft in case of disaster at sea and was some reassurance to the parents of our young crews. In port it became their dinghy if they wanted to do something on their own, as well as making a popular diving platform. Our old Walker trailing log was replaced with a Sumlog speed and distance instrument mounted on the wheelhouse shelf.

We were sufficiently confident in *Fairwater* now to attempt a trip to Scilly in the Spring bank holiday week, as well as our usual cruise in the Summer. After calling at St Mawes on Saturday we arrived in Scilly mid afternoon on Sunday May 25th. Our stay in Scilly was enlivened by the arrival of our friends the Hughes family in their 35 foot Laurence Giles sloop *Havssula* . We first met the Hughes family back in our *Vyaj* days and we had been instrumental in finding them a good riverside home opposite us on the Tamar at Saltash when Harry retired from British Airways. He sailed *Havssula* to Brittany and Spain and eventually took her across the Atlantic to the West Indies and back. They had not visited Scilly before, so we took some pride in being able to show them around some of the more useful channels. We returned up channel on Wednesday having to be back, without fail, ready for work after the coming weekend.

Day trips followed during June and the first half of July, the only one difference from normal routine being involved with the crowd of spectator craft to watch the start of the Round Britain race on Saturday July 6th.

Our Summer cruise was again destined for Scilly with our two nephews Andrew and Richard Davy and we got as far as Fowey on our first day, Friday July 19th. In the harbour we were pleased to see *Havssula* at anchor, but she was on her way home. We pushed on to St Mawes next day and on to the Isles of Scilly on Sunday, arriving at 17:30, later than planned as we met heavy drizzle and poor visibility over the last stages of the trip, coming in to the north of our intended route and having to come in cautiously before spotting the unmistakable silhouette of Hanjague and then having to push against the north running tide to come in through Crow Sound entrance. Once in the harbour the cold, damp and anxious crew were immediately revived with large helpings of delicious hot turkey stew which Peggy had prepared in the galley on the final stage of the trip.

We spent three days anchored in Tresco Channel in the lee of Bryher sheltering from westerlies forecast to reach force seven to eight. We passed the time walking, fishing and prawning. The catch of prawns was small but enough to decorate the lobster we bought from a cottage on Tresco. When the winds eased we went mackerel fishing around St Mary's. Another day was spent on St Agnes and another on Samson where we were pleased to raise anchor under sail, return to St Mary's harbour and re-anchor successfully in our favourite spot without using the engine at all.

On Sunday 25th we visited the Eastern Islands and St Martin's and on Monday with our friends the Pickups on board, we went around the Norrard Rocks, stopping for lunch in St Helen's Pool and returning to St Mary's after going around St Martin's and threading our way through the Eastern Islands.

By Wednesday 31st July we were thinking of the need to return home. We left St Mary's at 11:00 to 'have a look outside' but the sea was lumpy, the southwest wind was increasing and the barometer was dropping quickly, so we came back to anchor in the shelter of Watermill Cove and then back for the night to Tresco harbour where we would be sheltered if the wind reached gale force and turned into a westerly.

The next morning we left Tresco Channel at 06:45 with one of the crew still sound asleep in the fo'c'sle and headed out through Crow Sound towards Wolf Rock lighthouse with a now quite gentle westerly breeze and following seas to help us. From our departure from Hats Buoy off St Mary's to anchorage in the Helford river we only took nine hours and that included half an hour at low speed so the boys could catch some mackerel.

We left Helford Friday morning after a beautifully quiet night, enjoying breakfast in the sunshine in the wheelhouse and enjoying the ever delightful scenery. We called into St Mawes for shopping then reached Fowey harbour by 18:00 for the night.

Saturday saw us back in the Yealm for our traditional last night stop before returning home, including a celebration meal at the Old Ship as a farewell gesture to the crew.

Returning home on Sunday we could not fail to be pleased with this holiday. We had spent our longest period in the Islands (ten days) and had travelled around and in amongst them as never before. The weather had never settled into a calm spell but it had not produced bad gale conditions either. As usual we had anchored frequently without trouble, never picking up a mooring for the whole cruise. *Fairwater* was returning in good measure weeks of holiday to repay us for our weeks of work on her.

Later in the month with Peggy back at work and me still on holiday I suggested a few days 'minicruise' with Phil Robins, who was now no longer a little lad but had grown to 6'4" and seventeen stones and whose constant help with work on the boat deserved the reward of a cruise along the coast. Unfortunately the weather was wet and windy for all the five days in which we covered 127 miles at sea, going down to Falmouth and back.

We had a particularly wet and rough trip from Falmouth around the Dodman and into Fowey, where the rain was driving horizontally before a gale by the time we arrived in the harbour. Leaving on Monday, we returned for the traditional last evening ashore at Newton Ferrers. As we approached Rame Head, we did not see it until just before our E.T.A. because it was hidden in a thick blanket of fog which covered everything except the white water of the swell breaking on the rocks at the base of the cliffs. The strong winds of the previous day had gradually died and we could see a white double ended yacht with a brown gaff sail close by the rocks and halfway into Whitsand Bay. As we passed on our way to Penlee Point she fired a red distress flare and we turned back to help. Although there was then a Coastguard lookout at the top of Rame Head, he would not have been able to see the grass outside his windows, let alone a boat in trouble half a mile away and we had no radio transmitter.

We went to assist and found that their boat's engine had failed and they had lost their only anchor trying to keep off the rocks and the swell and lack of wind prevented her from beating out to sea away from the rocks. She was indeed almost on the rocks when we took her tow rope and gently took the strain to pull her clear. The first swell that buried her bow while our stern was lifting broke her tow rope and sent the deck fairlead on *Fairwater's* stern pinging high, high up into the air. Fortunately *Fairwater* had strong samson posts at the aft end of the cockpit and after clearing the remains of their elderly rope, we went back in and offered them a new, strong courlene warp of ours. This they gladly took, in spite of the salvage implications of having to be towed by another boat's equipment. We successfully towed them around Rame and past Penlee into the shelter of Cawsand where they could hang on to a buoy off Pier Cellars. Her crew were three young people they had just survived a very nasty (and potentially fatal) experience and they did not look the sort to have any spare money and possibly no insurance either.

To save them the worry of a salvage claim I shouted to them that the towage fee was a bottle of Scotch left behind the bar at the Royal Western Yacht Club. It was nearly Christmas before I had a phone call from the Secretary at the R.W.Y.C. to say that they had a mystery bottle with a label "To the crew of *Fairwater*" on it and did I know anything about it? No amount of money would have given me as much pleasure as the thought that the people we helped had gone to the trouble of honouring their towage fee.

Free of our tow we proceeded across the Sound and around the Mewstone in the fog for the traditional end of voyage visit to the Yealm and the Old Ship at Noss Mayo.

The atrocious weather persisted for most of the rest of the season but Phil and I did have one more trip, again on a wet and windy day, when we caught over 70 mackerel on our spinning lines, four dozen of which were selected for treatment in a homemade smoker (converted from an old oven) at the bottom of our garden. At least I had plenty of oak chips to provide the smoke, left over from making *Fairwater's* deck beams.

The rest of the season was mainly taken up by building a concrete block wall at the back of our quay to take half a dozen big pitch pine beams (most of which drifted in) on which we raised a new workshop, leaving the space underneath as a boat's gear store.

1975 was another year in which we made two trips to Scilly. The first being the Spring bank holiday half term week when Peggy and I gave ourselves the luxury of going to Scilly without taking any of our keen young crew members with us.

We left the mooring after work on Friday evening, my long suffering wife putting up with my impatience to get to sea at the first available minute passing the Dodman by clear moon light at 22:30 and thankfully dropping anchor off St Mawes at 30 minutes past midnight. What a way to spend a Friday evening after a hard week's work! We slept soundly for what was left of the night.

Saturday and Sunday were spent at Helford and St Mawes and we fitted in a visit to Peggy's brother's caravan at Trelawarren before leaving St Mawes at 07:20 on Monday for our run to Scilly. For most of the trip we were able to switch off the Kelvin wing engine and raise full sail instead, arriving at St Mary's at 15:45 with 61.5 miles recorded on the log to complete a record run of eight and a half hours.

After two days in Scilly we decided to head back on Thursday, ever mindful of possible delays on the way back and the overriding necessity to be back at work on Monday morning. We might have known that the English Channel would exact some retribution for our easy trip down. The forecast was for winds force 6 northeasterly, decreasing 4 to 5 and going northwesterly. This was bound to be unpleasant with headwinds to start with but once we reached Land's End and the wind decreased and turned northwesterly, we would enjoy shelter from the land and increasing assistance from following, rather than head, winds.

The forecast was accurate except for one small detail: instead of going from northeast to northwest, the wind went from northeast to southeast. This is the worst possible direction for anyone trying to get up channel. Easterlies raise steep nasty seas on the way down channel and off headlands like Land's End and even more so the Lizard, they rear up into bad tempered hollows and breaking crests and they throw vicious steep waves all the way from the Lizard into Falmouth, where you are beam on to them, as they rise steeply on meeting the shallowing waters off Black Head and the Manacles. The problem with yachting as compared with motoring is that there is no hard shoulder to pull into in case of trouble. Once we passed Land's End and conditions worsened there was no point in turning back. We throttled back to four knots and watched for every seventh wave or so when we had to throttle back even more to stop it running across the deck and possibly smashing the wheelhouse windows. Off Lizard, as always, the ledges of rock threw seas up in all directions. Each wave had to be assessed for direction as well as steepness and at times three or four breaking seas came at us from as many different directions at once, so that all we could do was slow right down, hang on and hope that *Fairwater's* beautiful seaworthy hull would ride the waves like a seagull. Which it did of course. We then had nearly four hours of rolling wildly in beam seas to Falmouth, having to repeat the demanding techniques needed at the Lizard when we passed Black Head and the Manacles. Although *Fairwater* answered every request made to her, turning the heavy rudder and juggling with engine controls is not the ideal occupation for a lady helmsman, so although in theory taking half hour watches at the wheel, it was my responsibility to take over when things were at their worst. Anyway, I got some thrills and enjoyment out of this where anyone sane tends to wish only for a quick and painless death. Eventually we arrived at St Mawes, nearly twelve hours out from Scilly, half as long again as it had taken to do the reverse trip. Next day I had difficulty walking as my toenails had bitten into my flesh as I had struggled to keep my footing at the wheel.

Needless to say, the next day had very light southwesterly winds which would have made the trip a pleasure, The rest of the run home via Fowey was routine and we picked up the mooring at home on Sunday evening (after calling at the Yealm) having covered 248 miles at sea.

Our Summer cruise to Scilly at the end of July began as a struggle against the usual southwesterly winds, often forecast force 6 or 7, occasionally 8. We did reach the shelter of Helford river after three days and were then stuck there in such strong winds that *Fairwater* for the first time ever dragged her anchor while we were ashore. *Fairwater* had been watched by a number of anxious boats moored nearby as she found her own way between them, without causing any damage (as far as we know) before anchoring herself firmly again about two hundred yards down river. On returning to the boat in her strange new position we took the unusual step of putting her on a mooring to prevent a repetition during the coming hours of darkness.

On the Thursday we tried a tentative run as far as the approaches to the Lizard to "see what it is like outside" in spite of discouraging weather forecasts. One glance at the raging lines of white water off the headland was enough to send us turning quickly back the way we had come in the shelter of the coastline. Suffice it to say that, having time on our hands we hoisted our modest sail area, switched off the engines and found we were achieving seven knots most of the way back to the Manacles, which is as fast as we might go under power. We sailed in to St Mawes to pick up supplies and then back to the shelter of Helford at 19:00. We had covered forty miles without getting any nearer to Scilly!

Overnight the wind appeared to lessen but it is difficult to judge in the superb shelter of the Helford. The forecast was for decreasing westerlies becoming variable with poor visibility later. We got under way at 07:30 and after a rather bumpy rounding of the Lizard crossed Mounts Bay in increasingly comfortable conditions. We passed Wolf Rock at 13:00 having covered 38 miles and hopes of good visibility were confirmed when young Andrew Davy claimed to have sighted St Martin's half an hour later and the sighting was confirmed as genuine, not just a mirage induced by the traditional prize of a packet of crisps for the first sighting. Visibility remained good all the way in through the short cut to the harbour through Crow Sound, coming to anchor at 16:10. This was close to our best run of eight and a half hours.

On Saturday we took the Pickups (including delightful Spaniel Smokey) around the 'back' of Samson, Bryher and Tresco and allowed *Fairwater* to go gently aground on the sand near Northwethal so that we could do some shrimping near Foreman's Island. The catch was small so we returned to *Fairwater* and she floated off again, where the galley crew had remained behind to prepare lunch.

We shifted our anchorage across to St Helen's and landed in the dinghy near the ruined pest house and climbed to the top of the island to admire the view. We returned to St Mary's to drop our guests off at the old quay and then went back to Tresco Channel to anchor in the lee of Bryher, sheltered from the westerly winds.

Sunday was a gloriously sunny day and after walking on Tresco to Cromwell's Castle we took dinghies, a sandwich lunch and the shrimp nets to Samson bar, where we had a much better catch than the day before. Hearing a good forecast in the evening we raised anchor once again and left Tresco Channel by its northern entrance and keeping well clear of the Kettle came back the other side of Tresco to anchor off Old Grimsby for the night.

After a flat calm night, with no cloud and good moonlight we left our solitary anchorage after the crew divided into a walking party, crossing Tresco to Carn Near and a boating party (Andrew Davy and myself) who were going to navigate there by sea and anchor there to pick the walkers up by dinghy. The navigational difficulties by sea proved minor to those of the land party who claimed to have struggled through bracken six feet high and were waylaid by a family of baby pheasants.

We returned to St Mary's harbour for lunch, having arranged to pick up two young friends, Paul and Nadia Williams and Derek and Smokey Pickup for a mackerel fishing trip around St Mary's in perfect Summer weather. With the Kelvin wing engine doing all the work, the youngsters divided into two rival teams of sports fishermen, excitedly catching about fifty after humanely throwing back all the uninjured small ones. The boys' delight with this lovely day was crowned when Peggy disappeared vertically into the clear waters of the harbour when losing her balance climbing out of the rubber dinghy.

Not content with all this activity for one day, we went across to St Agnes to anchor in Porth Conger at 19:00 and then moved around the island to the Cove, to anchor for the night. Andrew Hutchings concluded the entertainment of the day by falling backwards out of the dinghy, fully clothed, when we suddenly grounded on a small swell when landing on the Gugh sand bar.

Tuesday 29th July dawned with a continuation of the perfect weather. The Cove at St Agnes in these conditions seemed to be the most beautiful in all the Islands. The sandy beach ahead, the green banks of St Agnes on one side and the Gugh on the other with vivid patches of yellow gorse, sea pinks and weathered granite boulders opened on to a wide entrance to the east where the blue of the sky and the blue of the sea met on the distant horizon. The old white lighthouse overlooked the Cove, where terns dived on shoals of sparkling sand eels, clearly visible darting away in the crystal sea. Only a couple of other boats lay at anchor, well clear of each other, so we had this little bit of heaven almost exclusively to ourselves, before the tripper boats from St Mary's brought a scatter of walkers and sunbathers to the scene. Such perfection is usually referred to in *Fairwater's* log as a "Vintage Scillonian Day".

We had to leave the scene before mid morning, as our water tanks required filling from the quay at St Mary's harbour and we had another busy day with yesterday's crew on board again, going around the Eastern Islands, anchoring at Brandy Point, St Martin's and then landing at St Martin's quay for shopping when the tide rose sufficiently. Then back to drop our passengers at St Mary's before heading north for St Helen's Pool to anchor in solitary splendour for the night. All this running around to the western, northern and eastern limits of the island group only required twenty miles of travelling.

Wednesday was devoted to visiting two of the most atmospheric anchorages in the Isles of Scilly. Both are on the Eastern Islands and both have more than their fair share of archaeological remains. One is Little Arthur and the other Nornour.

Now I have to digress from the log of *Fairwater's* voyaging to try to put into words the world of mystery I feel around me when I visit these solitary, unspoilt islands.

Chapter Five

Legends and Theories

My love for the Islands is far from unique. So many visitors return, drawn by an instinct so deep that words to explain it are difficult to come by. The Islanders themselves, of course, feel even more strongly devoted. Seeing the seasons change as the years go by, many of them enjoy the Winter months best of all, when the visitors have virtually disappeared. Sadly, many Islanders have to leave for the Mainland to pursue careers and financial rewards and they feel the pull of the Islands most of all. What is equally sure is that this mystical attraction has haunted the Islands for centuries before recorded time. Apart from the beauty of the scenery, there has always been a feeling that there is some holy, religious significance about the Islands. Even the strange shapes and enormous size of the outcrops of granite provide the atmosphere of an enduring natural cathedral.

The Islands also have a closeness to the sun, the sea and the tempestuous forces of nature, placing them on the threshold of the great mystery of what goes on when human life ends. The feeling that the Islands were sacred in pre Christian times is evident from the number of ancient burial sites abounding there, usually commanding viewpoints over the sea, facing west towards the setting sun. The entrances and passageways of most of the tombs face east but I feel these are 'back doors' to sites chosen to face west. So many of these monuments situated within such a small area, compared with similar sites on the nearby Mainland, indicate that they were not just graveyards for local people but were for the illustrious dead of the Celtic tribes of Brittany, Ireland, Wales, Northern Spain and South West England. The isolation of the Islands, twenty five miles from Land's End in the Atlantic swells and cross currents of the English Channel made burial there an act of some importance. Added to that was the labour involved in transporting, shaping and assembling the ponderous slabs and blocks of granite involved. This activity implies an hierarchy of planners and organizers demanding the respect and fear of the local tribesmen who would have to do all the hard work. So there must have been a caste of powerful priests, perhaps the shadowy Druids, respected for their wisdom and feared for their ruthless power. There is some logic in adding a cult of priestesses who probably began the Island tradition of the wise 'Aunts' famed for their medical skills in more recent centuries. Further mention of this possibility will be made later.

With this background the Isles of Scilly would naturally attract a reputation for being sacred or holy. This might provide a clue to the derivation of the name for the Isles. In the Middle Ages in England the word "silly" had a far different meaning from today. One instance of this comes from the time of King James I, when he wrote his book on the theory on the Divine Right of Kings. He used the word "silly" to mean extremely sacred and holy. He described himself as "God's silly vassal". It is easy to see how over recent centuries the word has changed its meaning from holy to lacking in practical common sense and finally to a gentle form of stupidity. How far back the word 'silly' kept to its original meaning I do not know but 'The Silly Isles' simply meaning 'The Holy Isles' has a strong ring of logic about it.

Why should this scatter of tiny islands become so important to the peoples of the 'Celtic Fringe'? The answer lies in the geography of the lines of communication between England, France, Ireland, Wales and Spain. What limited amount of trading there was between these related peoples had to go by sea. Put the routes on the map, e.g. Brittany to Ireland or Spain to Cornwall and Scilly emerges as a natural crossroads, with its geographic significance added to by its notorious reputation for rocks and currents demanding respect from the primitive craft and seamanship of the time. One only has to look at the vapour trails of today's huge passenger airliners criss crossing overhead or look out to sea at the shipping following the separation lanes between the Islands and Land's End to realize that the geographic significance still exists today. Going back in time from the trails in the sky today, firm evidence exists of the trade routes from Scilly to parts of the Celtic Fringe in the form of flint adzes from the Gimble Porth area on Tresco. These adzes are earlier than 3000 BC and made from Welsh flint. It is appropriate that these flint tools are forerunners of the adzes which are still today essentially a boat builders tool. So trade routes to and boat building on Scilly can confidently be believed to go back for more than 5000 years.

The burial structures are so prolific, so varied in style and mostly so difficult of access that even the vast amount of archaeological research spent on them tends to complicate the subject, rather than clarify it. My layman's method of coming to an understanding of them is that there are three basic types. The biggest are the 'burial chambers', of which there are three different patterns, the 'cyst graves', basically four slabs of stone set at right angles with a fifth slab as a cover and 'burial cairns', which are, more crudely, piles of boulders to mark a single grave. As a vague guide, evidence exists for about fifty each of the first two types and about four hundred for the third. The Islands can be proud to have three times as many of the big chambered tombs as the whole of Cornwall.

The only justification for building the big chambered tombs, is that having built a stone structure for the remains and relics of the dead, the passageway to the chamber could be sealed off to prevent casual invasion of the site, but it would be available at an appropriate time to be opened to receive an unlimited number of remains, especially if these were in the form of ashes from a cremation put into a pottery urn. There are always exceptions to every rule: the burial chamber at Bant's Carn was obviously the resting place for the earthly remains of the people who lived there and was a deeply significant part of the community spirit there. But the procession of burial chambers on the ridges of the smaller islands such as Samson and Gugh, some ten to twelve approximately on each, cannot be justified by the number of inhabitants of these small areas, but could be explained if a cult existed for the import of remains of the illustrious dead from the whole spread of the Celtic Fringe. Another element that might have contributed to the shape of the 'passage tombs' is the symbolic shape of the womb and the birth canal through which all human life comes naturally into the world. The Celtic religious respect for the 'trinity of fertility' i.e. the process of (i) Birth (ii) Death and (iii) Return to Mother Earth to be reborn would logically find expression in the design of the tomb representing the return of the dead to the womb of Mother Earth via a narrow passageway. Fragments of pottery, dating back to 3000 years BC link the burial chambers of Scilly with those of Cornwall. The care and skill put into this pottery, with a tradition of similar forms found in Cornwall, with the decoration, achieved by impressing twisted or plaited cord in a zigzag pattern points to a tradition of the import of remains to a Celtic sacred site. Lacking any written evidence, this belief requires some faith and imagination.

Then, when written evidence does emerge, everything still points to the Isles of Scilly as somewhere with sacred, or holy, connotations. Mediterranean civilizations, Greek, Phoenician or Roman, all benefited from sophisticated written languages and accounts were recorded in them of geographical, religious and economic importance. Rival Mediterranean cultures fought with each other. The Greeks destroyed the Persians, the Romans destroyed the Carthaginians: all for trade, empire and wealth. But the key to success for their armed forces depended not only on the military traditions of their fighting men but also upon the quality of their weapons and armour. To achieve the right durability they needed bronze; to make bronze they needed tin; to obtain tin they had to travel as far as Cornwall; to navigate to Cornwall from Spain or Brittany they needed to know about the

Isles of Scilly. It follows that the first written references to Scilly come from the Mediterranean in Greek or Latin.

Most history books tell us that the Phoenicians traded for tin with the 'Cassiterides', the tin islands. It is easy to believe that this term describes Scilly, West Cornwall and St Michael's Mount. There is no proof that the Phoenician merchants ever came in fleets of ships from the Mediterranean through the Straits of Gibraltar then along the Atlantic coast of Portugal and Spain, finally to face the Bay of Biscay and the difficult waters around Scilly and Cornwall in order to trade for tin. They would then have to face the perils of the return trip. They had no need for such hazardous sailing.

They had a base in the port of Marseilles (Masala?) and overland transport routes existed to go across France to Brittany. These tracks would not be suitable for wheeled transport, but a string of packhorses, well defended and guided by local knowledge, could take trade goods comparatively quickly and safely overland to within easy reach of the English Channel and Cornwall where the precious tin could be obtained.

A justification for this theory comes from the ingot of tin salvaged from the sea off St Mawes. It was cast in the shape of the letter 'H'. There must be good reason why the Cornish tinners went to the extra trouble of casting ingots with this shape. Put a round rock under the crossbar of the 'H' and bend it by hammering and you have a convenient shape for putting on the back of a packhorse. Written evidence exists that the tin trade from Cornwall crossed the Channel and rounded Brittany to the port of Cobilo at the mouth of the river Loire before continuing through the Bay of Biscay to the Garonne river. Here the horse transport took over for an overland journey of about thirty days through the Carcassone Pass to Narbonne and finally to Marseilles.

I personally believe that over many centuries BC the Isles of Scilly had a special significance for three reasons: they were the Holy Islands dedicated to the burial of the Celts: they were of crucial importance to the seafarers of the Celtic Fringe who traded between Spain, Brittany, Cornwall, Wales and Ireland and they had a geographic and navigational significance for the annual tin trade between the Phoenician merchants and the Cornish tinners.

What tangible proof is there of this extraordinary importance? Let us look at the fascinating island of Nornour in the Eastern Island group. Following storm damage in the 1920's a settlement was revealed, which when excavated, produced well preserved walls of numerous round houses, with their door posts, fire places and querns for grinding corn. This settlement nestled in the shelter of a steep hill and the excavation produced an amazingly rich hoard of valuable objects. Apart from numerous rings and coins, there were nearly three hundred decorative brooches, of the type used to fasten the gowns of the Celtic womenfolk of some importance. They are of such diverse style of construction and decoration that they must have been brought to Nornour by sea, rather than having been manufactured on the spot. These brooches have an unmistakable feminine style to them and one possible logical explanation of the hoard is that the buildings housed a cult of priestesses and the brooches were votive offerings made to them by seafarers from the Celtic Fringe of Europe. If we accept a cult of Druids to organize the burials it would not be surprising to find an associated cult of priestesses nearby, whose function would have little to do with the burial chambers, but could well have a separate function linked with the sea and the shipping which we can be sure visited or passed close to Scilly. Some solid written proof for this theory comes from the final destruction of the resistance to the Roman army led by the last of the Druids, recorded as happening in Anglesey (part of the Celtic Fringe) in AD 61, by Tacitus. The Roman soldiery, who were a very tough and experienced lot, admitted to being terrified by the sight of long haired, black robed women among the opposing ranks, chanting and screaming curses and hatred; significantly they carried blazing torches.

Another tradition of the existence of black robed priestesses in South West England comes from Arthurian legend. When King Arthur was mortally wounded in his last tragic battle with Mordred he was taken from the Cornish coast on a ship crewed by priestesses dressed in black. These black robes may have been something unique to Scilly. In the 1st century AD Strabo, writing in Latin, described the men inhabiting the Cassiterides as "wearing black cloaks, clad in tunics reaching to the feet, girt about the breast and walking with staves." This makes an interesting contrast to the tradition that the Ancient Britons were associated with the colour blue and the vegetable die woad that produced it. These references to black robes show that there was something unusually significant about the colour at the time. If it were part of the ritual associated with the use of Scilly as one of the Holy sites of the Celtic Fringe, then we should not be surprised that priests and monks of the Christian faith which superseded the old Celtic religion frequently copied the long black robes, prominently belted, as a powerful religious symbol. Even the Bishop's and Archbishop's 'crooks' may have found their origin with the black robed inhabitants of the 'Holy Isles' who, remarkably, "walked with staves." These two glimpses of this cult indicate that (a) such a cult existed, (b) that fire played a part in their ritual activities and (c) that they performed medical assistance associated with ships. Now, if the cult of black robed priestesses was based on Nornour it would not be surprising if they accumulated a hoard of brooches with which to fasten their robes and these would be a natural gift to offer them by the seafarers for whom they had provided help, hospitality and medical services in these Islands at the crossroads of the shipping routes of the time.

If such a theory sounds far fetched, why are two islands, very close to Nornour in the Eastern Islands called Great Arthur and Little Arthur, when all the rest of them have names with a distinctly different sound to them?. Could not the black robed priestesses who took King Arthur to his final resting place have been those based on Nornour? Amongst the Ganinicks, the Ganillys, Hanjague, the Innisvouls and Menawethan, how do we suddenly find a comparatively modern and prosaic name such as Arthur? And on Little Arthur, overlooking the Island group towards Samson and the setting Atlantic sun, why is there a quite magnificent cyst grave? Who knows?

The trail to find a cult of priestesses on Nornour does not go cold at this stage. Yet another mysterious reference from ancient written history tends literally to shed more light on the subject. The Greek explorer Pytheas circumnavigated the British Isles three centuries BC and recorded the name of Land's End as Bolerium. Roman navigators four centuries later still used the same word, when for instance, Ptolemy of Alexandria, a renowned geographer, gave a list of capes and headlands around Britain and when he came to Land's End, he still called it Bolerium but he prefixed it with the word antivestaeum. This has to translate easily as "opposite the light". It also implies through "vesta" a light dedicated to the Roman goddess who was always served by vestal virgins, devoted to the fires of the hearth and the provision of light.

The importance of a light on Scilly to aid the navigators of the Celtic Fringe is obvious. Today, with satellite navigational systems, radars, depth sounders etcetera, Scilly still demands to be circled with light. The Bishop, the Wolf, Round Island, the Seven Stones and Peninnis lights still flash their warnings and provide useful points of reference to today's shipping.

Going back centuries BC, the provision of a light all the year around would be preposterous. But in the Summer months and when the generously financed tin trade with Cornwall would take place annually at a time mutually convenient to the Phoenician merchants and their Celtic ships and seamen, how valuable would be a light, when the sea journeys at low speeds in primitive craft would necessitate voyaging at night.

Where would be the ideal site for a brazier, fuelled by wood? Obviously at the eastern end of the Islands on a prominent hill with access to loads of oak logs (carbon dating research shows that ancient Scilly had an abundance of oak forests) tended by dedicated people who would in turn be rewarded by the seafarers concerned for help in the past and encouraged to keep the system going in the future. Today Nornour is separated from Great Ganilly by a shallow ledge of rock, which in the times mentioned above, would have been flat fields giving access to the hill on Great Ganilly, which is the steepest, highest hill in the Eastern Islands, marked on today's maps as 110 feet. What do we find at the top of that hill? A cairn of rocks. Scilly abounds with burial chambers, cyst graves, standing stones and numerous funeral cairns, but a solitary cairn of respectable size on the top of a hill is an exception, not a rule.

Around this cairn is a perfect circle of bare rock and soil, on a horizontal site. Heading up the hill to this site, which looks ideal for a bonfire, is, in terms of the Scillonian Off Islands, a reasonably wide and even approach track, not waist deep in bracken and brambles as might be expected. Bracken and brambles flourish on old, cultivated ground, but perhaps here we have a primitive road, with sufficiently firm foundation to provide access for the necessary supplies of wood to provide a primitive light in the middle of the circle at the top of the hill.

So we have a site for the light. We have a need for a light. We have written reference to a light opposite Land's End. We have encouraging reason to believe that a cult of priestesses linked to the Roman goddess of light might have provided this service. We have a settlement where they would have lived on Nornour. Finally we have a possible explanation for the hoard of brooches found buried in that site.

When we go back to a few centuries AD and some millenniums BC to picture the existence of this site, we have to bear two or three things in mind. Firstly, we know that the Eastern Islands, St Martin's, Tresco and St Mary's were all one large island, known as Ennor. Secondly, with its background as an Holy Island we would expect quite a number of holy sites to be scattered about, e.g. Holy Vale, and if we want to look for them, we might best be advised to look at the Christian sites which probably succeeded the original Celtic site. The granite Roman altar stone now in Tresco Abbey proves the Roman link. An Arthurian link with Tresco is possible if only because of the quaintly named Appletree Bay which appears devoid of apple trees. In Arthurian times, the sandy Tresco Flats which cover a huge area between Tresco, Samson and Bryher which today is covered by the beautifully coloured sea at all but low Spring tides, would have been an area of low lying fertile land, quite suitable for growing orchards of apple trees. The Celtic name for such a "Vale of Apples" could well be translated as "Avalon" where it would enjoy the kindly climate associated with Tresco Abbey and Appletree Bay today. Just the word "Avalon" evokes the idea of a peaceful, desirable place of holy significance to Arthurian legend.

Among the last remnants of the apple trees, bee hives suggest that honey was another useful crop harvested by the Celts and then the Christians on the Abbey site on Tresco. The Celts from about 1500 to 1000 BC have become identified as the 'Beaker' period, from their custom of placing ritual drinking vessels in the graves. Apples and honey both produce well known varieties of alcoholic drinks. These traditional crops, so close to the Christian Abbey site suggest that the Abbey could have been a site of religious significance to the Celtic Beaker people long before the monks of Tavistock Abbey arrived. When the monks did arrive, they introduced the elder trees which could withstand sand and salt better than apple trees. Could it be that the monks used the elder flowers to flavour the traditional mead and cider (or combination of the two) or that they harvested the rich purple berries to make elderberry wine. The old Beaker people would not find it too surprising to find the ceremonial use of wine at the heart of the Christian communion service.

Just one more coincidence leads me to believe in the importance of the Nornour/Ganilly site on the Eastern Islands. This is linked with the legend of the great inundation of Lyonesse, when some natural catastrophe occurred which brought its importance to an end. The story of this great flood lived in the folk tales of numerous generations of illiterate people living in Cornwall before William of Worcester visited the area and put the oral traditions into print for the first time. This written account refers to the inundation of one hundred and forty parish churches, no doubt a poetic exaggeration to express the tragic consequences of the flood. But he also names three noblemen who, dramatically, barely escaped the raging sea and we know he was right about two of them because the Trevelyans and the Vyvyans both have waves and white horses on their coats of arms which form part of Cornish local history. The third nobleman has always been a puzzle because of the difficulty of tracing the Lord of Goonhilly; apart from the fact that the bare heathland close to the Lizard headland is a most unlikely area of land to support a noble family. But the island of Ganilly in the Scillies, with the importance attached to it because of its religious and seafaring associations which I have suggested, might indeed have been wealthy enough to warrant a titled leader. Ganilly and Goonhilly are just alternate spellings for a Celtic word meaning a salt wind blasted heathland. Some confirmation of this theory comes from the fact that the story of his survival pinpoints the place where he came safely to land as Sennen Cove: the closest Mainland port of arrival from Scilly.

If further proof of this event is needed, this Lord of Ganilly built a chapel at Sennen Cove in gratitude for his survival. It was called Chapel Idne and its crude, but substantial construction was recorded on early photographs. Now, unhappily, it has been destroyed to provide car parking space. Sic Transit Omnia.

It is quite easy to mock the stories of the great flood and the inundation of Lyonesse, because the name itself seems to have no Celtic provenance. It is easy to commit Lyonesse and its inundation to the world of legend and romance. But let us look across to Brittany, as part of the Celtic Fringe and we find that on the extreme end of the Breton Peninsula, which ends with the Finisterre equivalent of Land's End, we find that today the closest province to Scilly is Leon. Now, Daphne du Maurier, when she went to Brittany to trace the roots of the du Maurier family, found a tradition that the bodies of the dead seafarers were collected mysteriously to be laid to rest in Holy Islands off the coast of Leon. If we take the Celtic word for island, enys (as in Peninnis in Scilly, Pen= headland, innis, of the island) and we add it to the province from which the dead were transported, we come up with Leonenys. Bearing in mind that spelling was an unknown science to the Celts at the time, it is very easy to see how pronouncing Leonenys could easily have an alternative spelling as Lyonesse.

Tradition has it that Lyonesse was engulfed by a catastrophic flooding. Not the gentle, almost imperceptible eustatic rise of the sea or the isostatic drop of the land so brilliantly described by Professor Thomas. Earthquakes are rare in Cornwall, but they do occur, as in the St Michael's Mount area on 10th November 1996. We do know that one earthquake was recorded at St Michael's Mount on the 11th September 1275, because it destroyed the well built church on the island so thoroughly that it could not be repaired, but had to wait for a rebuild in the following century. William of Worcester visited St Michael's Mount in 1478, almost exactly two centuries after this event and collected his stories from the oral traditions of the locals. It could possibly be that this earthquake, so severe that it passed into local folklore, was the one that devastated the populated areas of the Eastern Islands, altering the geography and leaving the scatter of small islands we see today in place of the larger single island of earlier times.

Other settlements at Porthcressa, Porthmellon, Tresco Channel and St Martin's Flats must have perished as well. The island possibly called 'Lethosow', with its few habitations became the Seven Stones Reef and the forest of trees around St Michael's Mount was washed away, leaving only the stumps and roots exposed by stormy Spring tides, for which photographic evidence exists today.

My amateur ramblings into the academic world of archaeology are only put forward as possibilities to explain the wealth of historical evidence underfoot and all around every visitor to the Islands. Add to everything in this chapter so far the much more recent Garrison Walls, the Star Castle, uniquely well preserved, Cromwell's Castle and King Charles' Castle on Tresco and the evocative remains of granite cottages on the exposed ridge of

Samson and they all add up to a treasure of historical remains beyond compare. They sit there for the enjoyment of those with eyes to see and imagination to wonder at their variety and richness, without having to pay an entry fee, which would be demanded on the Mainland for a simulated theme park of much more prosaic provenance.

As the years went by and our annual visits to the Islands rose beyond the thirty mark, the fascination always increased and the beauty of them and their timeless stories and legends became more obsessive with the passage of time.

Eastern Islands Magic

In the Islands of Scilly, just once in a while,
Some magic occurs on one small special Isle.
On a short night in Summer and rare to be seen,
The sea turns to purple and the moon turns to green.

On the Island of Nornour the Spirits arise,
Fair priestesses dance, their arms raised to the skies
And magical music from nowhere appears,
Sounds of seasurf sighing seduces their ears.

Their libations of mead send them off in a trance
And then all around them, Eastern Isles start to dance.
Little Ganilly trips forward with her silver sandy train
Heading for Little Arthur to hold him again.

Ganilly gavottes in his own stately measure
While the two Innisvouls start jigging together.
Hanjague stands on guard: he's too solid to move,
While Ganninnicks embrace, so close is their love.

Hard Lewis rocks, while Menawethan sways in the race
While with music and mead the dance goes on apace.
Before Dawn raises a finger, all movement must cease
And the Isles must return to their right state of peace.

If you think that I'm lying, or crazy perhaps,
Go back a few centuries and look at the maps.
Some Isles' names have changed, and it's not just by chance
They lost their way home at the end of the Dance!

Chapter Six

We returned to St Mary's and enjoyed a meal ashore in the home of two of our closest friends, Alba and Roger Williams, the parents of the two young crew members who had sailed with us during the past week.

Thursday was a rest day in port at St Mary's and Friday was a return to the Eastern Islands, before dinner ashore with the Pickups. By the end of the meal the lifeboat maroons exploded overhead and the boys were granted permission to rush down to the slip to see the lifeboat hit the water. Later we saw her winched up again when we were back on *Fairwater* and we learned that she had returned from a sad mission to help a holed St Mary's fishing boat which filled and sank off Tean before help arrived, having been damaged while working the notoriously dangerous Sevenstones Reef.

Saturday the 7th of August was crew change over day. Peggy had to return to work and she took the boys with her to Penzance on the *Scillonian* where Phil met her and left his car with her for the trip home, while he came back on the *Scillonian's* return trip to join me on *Fairwater* for a few days stay in Scilly and a cruise back to Plymouth.

On Sunday we moved to Tresco Channel so Phil could visit both Tresco and Bryher and we enjoyed a pasty for lunch at the New Inn. The wind strengthened overnight with heavy rain and we had a thunderstorm at breakfast time Monday morning, which lasted an hour. Later in the morning we left Tresco Channel by the north entrance, coming back through Old Grimsby Channel to circumnavigate the Island and then went on to Porth Conger so that Phil could add St Agnes to his list of islands visited. We also compared lunch at the Turk's Head there with yesterday's as part of his survey of the Islands' essential services. We went back to St Mary's in the late afternoon in beautiful sunshine, which returned the next day but with an increasing southerly wind behind it. For Tuesday, Phil added Little Arthur in the Eastern Islands to bring his total to five islands visited and we had to be content with passing Great Ganilly, Nornour and St Martin's close to, without stopping to land. Then back to harbour where we spent a rolly night with a strong south to southwest wind pushing a swell into the anchorage beam on to the way we were lying. We intended returning to the Mainland on Wednesday but the early shipping forecast gave occasional force eight winds for West Sole, which might be well out into the Atlantic from Scilly, but might logically send the winds in our direction later in the day.

By 09:30 after a leisurely breakfast the wind had died down to about force three from the southwest and the barometer was slowly rising, so we presumed the bad weather had passed. We raised anchor at 10:00 to see "what it was like outside". This quotation comes from a story about a legendary fishing village in Cornwall, where the fishermen found the answer to weather forecasting before the days of radio or television. They would give the weather a 'candle test' in the early morning, lighting a candle and taking it out of the cottage "to see what it was like outside". If the candle blew out they would tell their wives that there was too much wind to go to sea safely and if it did not blow out they told them there was not enough wind to sail.

We found (without the aid of a candle) that although sea conditions were lumpy, the seas from the leftover gale were in the right direction, coming from almost directly behind and lifting *Fairwater's* elegantly pointed stern gently but firmly on our way up channel. We passed Wolf Rock at 13:45 and made steady progress past Mounts Bay towards Lizard. Before we reached it, that wicked headland played another trick on us. It disappeared from view and sent squalls of heavy drizzle towards us from an offshore direction, so that we literally 'lost our bearings' and without the modern aids of autopilot and Decca navigation plotter which we enjoy today, presented us with a problem we had not anticipated. I steered up channel keeping to the course we had set to clear the Lizard but the problem was to decide when to make a right angled turn into Falmouth Bay, when the rocks of the Lizard were safely astern. Most Cornish headlands drop dramatically into deep clear water and are safe to approach closely. The Lizard is different. It gets its name from a long reef of triangular rocks that extend a long way out to sea and then an even longer distance relatively close to the surface. Hence the name because the series of rocks are like the back of a monster lizard, wriggling out to sea, with a long set of dorsal fins on its back, reminiscent of the most nightmarish of dinosaurs. The full Channel tides rush over the deadly ridge, throwing steep pyramids of water in all directions, which have to be seen to be believed from a small boat. If a contrary strong wind blows in an opposite direction to the current, the pyramids become steeper and closer, until their tops break, many feet in the air and fall vertically on any mariner unfortunate enough to be anywhere near them. They weigh many tons, they are heartless and they are very unfriendly.

The only safe thing to do is to avoid the whole scene by going five miles or more off the point, but if you are going to Falmouth you still have to turn towards the land and go through an area marked with 'overfalls' on the Admiralty chart. Although our wind was offshore and only moderate, the Lizard also has a 'headland effect' which always increases the windspeeds in its immediate area. Add thick drizzle with limited visibility and it can be easily understood why Phil and I had become a little anxious.

In a state of anxiety, time seems to slow down in comparison with the speed it races past when you are enjoying yourself. I was sure we were well past the dreaded headland and was getting a bit depressed by the atmosphere of gloom added to the effects of long hours of engine noise and seven hours of lurching and rolling up channel. My satisfaction with steering north turned to horror when cliffs well down channel from the Lizard loomed out of the murk and I could see the deadly white water of the Lizard race out to sea from our position. Turning through one hundred and eighty degrees and heading out to sea we were still pushed into the race by the speed of the tide behind us. The nightmare that followed was mercifully shortened by that same strong tide pushing us through. A lesser vessel than *Fairwater* could well have been damaged or overwhelmed. In spite of the miserably cold weather I became uncomfortably hot with sweat that was not entirely caused by fear, but resulted from the effort needed to control the steering wheel and try to turn *Fairwater's* bow into the steepest seas, which gave very few seconds notice of their approach. Phil hung on in the cockpit with both hands to avoid being thrown around and wisely kept his head down to avoid looking at the nastiness around us. At last, by 17:45, we were through the worst of it and could steer for Black Head and then on to St Anthony lighthouse before coming to anchor off St Mawes at 20:30. This was Phil's first passage from Scilly to Falmouth and, as he said, he had no idea it could last so long!

As often happens after a bad trip, the next day was beautifully sunny with a gentle breeze and excellent visibility. We were driven back on board for a sandwich lunch in the cool, after shopping in St Mawes in blazing sunshine. In the afternoon we part sailed and part motored across to Helford where after an evening meal on board, I was able to introduce Phil to the delights of the Shipwright's Arms in the evening.

The next day, Friday August 8th, started with passing thunderstorms and heavy showers which persisted all the morning. With some signs of clearance midday we raised our anchor with some difficulty from underneath the anchor chain of a large motor sailer that had anchored too close to us and were just merrily heading down river, when sudden clanking and banging noises from under the cockpit floor forced us to pick up the nearest mooring buoy and investigate the problem. The prop shaft coupling bolts were all loose and the grub screw not holding. Yesterdays hectic manoeuvring with sudden changes of engine revs had no doubt caused the problem. We blessed *Fairwater* for waiting until calm waters and handy mooring buoys to finally break down, instead of in the worst of the Lizard race the day before!

On leaving Helford entrance we were buffeted by a stiff northwesterly breeze with renewed thundery showers. We headed for the comfort of St

Mawes instead of struggling up channel. I got thoroughly soaked that evening going ashore in the dinghy to phone home with our present position.

We left St Mawes early next morning with the wind moderated to northwest force three but the sky was overcast with heavy showers in the distance. We were heading for Fowey but after passing the Dodman at 10:30, we decided to use the favourable northwest wind to motorsail up channel and head for the Tamar. At 13:00, some distance from Rame Head we decided to switch off the diesel and enjoy a sandwich lunch in peace and quiet and trail a mackerel line so that we could take a little present of fresh fish home to our relatives and friends. By the time we reached Rame we caught forty, with the sea alive with surfacing mackerel and flocks of gannets diving to share in the feast.

Pleased with this lucky homecoming, we ran up the Tamar to pick up our mooring at Saltash Passage at 16:45. Since leaving the mooring three weeks before, we had covered 406 miles at sea.

We only had one or two day trips over the remainder of the season, because of a heavy work load ashore. We bought an electric concrete mixer and I built two covered bunkers for sand and gravel beside a shed (always referred to at home as the 'site office') where cement was stored in the dry, and power points and water supply were installed. The object was to complete work in the garden on terracing and wall building and an extension of our grid on the beach, with a wall against the cliff facing out towards the river, with a dozen railway sleepers as fendering. We were not to know at the time how vital these beach facilities were to be over the coming Winter, because for the second time in her life, *Fairwater* was to be swept from her mooring in a storm and threatened with destruction against the rough stonework of a quay.

Work continued relentlessly over the Christmas holiday and during the week leading up to Friday January 2nd. Phil, being on holiday, was available to help. We finally exhausted ourselves on the Friday by shovelling, wheelbarrowing and stowing a six ton lorry load of gravel in the bunker at the end of the path from the side gate where the load had been dumped on the pavement. We were used to working in rough weather conditions but a howling gale set in that blew my cap off five times, twice going over the high wall into the road as I pushed the wheelbarrow along. After the load was stored and I cleaned myself up and relaxed to enjoy a well earned weekend, the doorbell rang and instead of the friend I expected to call in for a friendly drink and chat, the son of the local boatbuilder stood with rain pouring off him to announce that *Fairwater* had broken her mooring and was smashing herself broadside on to the quay of the Tamar River Sailing Club.

I rang Phil, who immediately drove down to assist, much as he needed some rest. Peggy joined us to rush, clad in oilskins, to the quay, which for security reasons was locked against us and we climbed over walls and fences to find *Fairwater* rolling and crashing against the quay, held there by storm force winds and a steep sea ploughing down the Lynher river with about two miles of 'fetch' behind it. We could climb on board and put a few fenders out, but they would do nothing to prevent *Fairwater* being thrown bodily against the quay by the seas and simultaneously having her keel and rudder pounded on the beach as she rose and fell. The alternatives were simple: we could either drive her along the quay and out into the river, or we could leave her where she was and watch her being smashed up. We could already see the hull flexing and straining as it hit the quay and we could hear and see the judder go through her as she was bounced on the beach. The problem was that with the best of intentions we had brought the starting batteries ashore for trickle charging and they were on our quay, at the bottom of a steep path, several hundred yards down river. Phil and I raced back over the fence and wall to the road, back to our house and down the steps to the quay. We disconnected the batteries, which were so heavy that we normally carried one between us, picked them up, climbed all the way back to the road, carrying one each and how we lifted them over the wall and the fence and on board where they had to be stowed below the cockpit floor beams and connected to the starting cables with all the lurching and crashing going on, I just do not know. Peggy had bravely remained on the quay, buffeted by the gale and rain, trying with her bare hands to ease the smashing of the hull against the quay. The damage this did to her arms, neck and shoulders gave her painful reminders over the years to come.

At panic speed I started the engine (good old reliable Commodore) and with nothing to lose but our lives I drove her firmly, but without too much helm along the quay and out into the river. The darkness was accentuated by the pouring rain but somehow we steered through the moorings into the middle of the river, where we could head out into the storm at slow speed and assess the damage. Quite likely she was making so much water that she might sink, in which case I would head at full speed for the more sheltered side of the river at Saltash and hope to find a reasonably soft beach to drive her ashore.

Much use of the 'Whale Gusher' bilge pump eventually began to suck air, so we could remain afloat but now I had to decide what to do with no dinghy, no mooring and the storm still driving up river.

On the Saltash side, with a sheltered beach and a boathouse lived our friend Harry Hughes, so we headed towards it and anchored off, having seen Harry appear at his boathouse door, dressed for action and carrying a good storm lantern, having guessed that the vessel he had seen in distress from his house could only have been ours.

We still had the problem of putting *Fairwater* in on his beach. We anchored just off Coombe Creek for the necessary operations. Firstly we had to bolt on *Fairwater's* legs, so that once ashore she would sit upright on the beach. Bolting these on in the dark in a gale was not easy but at least we were at anchor. Then we had to lay an anchor out in the creek to become a stern mooring so that *Fairwater* would sit on the beach without going sideways or crash bow on into Harry's boathouse. Our kedge anchor was taken from its stowage and lifted on deck with its chain and heavy warp. Then we had to lift our main anchor, edge *Fairwater* into the creek at low engine revs and anchor again so that we were over the spot where the kedge anchor ought to be. Then we could drop the kedge, retrieve our main anchor and gently head for the boathouse until we could cast a line ashore and pull ahead on the bowline so that we could just step ashore on to Harry's quay, paying out on the kedge anchor warp to keep her under complete control.

Harry's wife Pam, who had also turned up in oilskins to assist, took a battered and exhausted Peggy and Phil back across the bridge to Saltash Passage. Harry and I waited for *Fairwater* to take the ground and between 23:00 and midnight we laid out more secure stern moorings and at 05:00 we went down to pick up Harry's creek mooring lines and hauled *Fairwater* exactly where we wanted her as the tide rose again.

Later in the day we examined the hull for damage, unbelievably little in view of the pounding she had taken. The brass rubbing band on the starboard side had disappeared and the sturdy pitch pine rubber behind it was badly chafed in places, but not broken. There were extensive areas of paintwork that had been scarred by the rough stonework of the quay, but the fenders and Peggy's valiant efforts in fending her off had prevented the damage getting to the planking under the paintwork. The saddest thing was the general weakening of the planking and seams around the already weakened sternpost area, which had taken the force of the pounding on the beach. No time for tears, but a routine fitting out would only put a cosmetic layer over the hidden damage. We had to start all over again by putting *Fairwater* on the grid, jacking her up above the high tide mark and recruiting an experienced shipwright to assess the extent of the damage and put it right, presuming it was possible to do so.

Much hard work had to be faced to achieve this. *Fairwater* still had her masts and cruising equipment on board. All this had to be removed, plus her ton and a half of ballast blocks. The work on the grid had to be finished to take her and then we had to jack her up and secure her so that planking could be removed if necessary. The main mast was lifted out at Saltash and stored in the boathouse together with a load of other gear and *Fairwater* was moored on our beach, ready for a suitable tide to put her on the grid. The ballast blocks, anchors, chain and other heavy gear were put ashore and we tried to put her on the grid on the evening of Sunday 18th January. The 5.5 metre tide was not quite enough. On Monday, before work, we were down on the slip at 07:00 for a 5.7 metre tide and in calm water and moonlight we were able to put her two thirds of the way up the slip and a repeat performance the next morning, with the water level raised by a southwesterly gale, we were able to warp her into a satisfactory position on the new slip. Once again *Fairwater* had been saved from destruction but could she ever be made thoroughly seaworthy again?

Once more the right man for the job came along. Arthur Keith was an ex Navy shipwright, now instructing apprentices in the dockyard. He agreed to undertake the repair in his spare time. Once *Fairwater* was jacked up and secured two feet above the grid, Arthur patiently removed all the fastenings from the after ends of the planks where they were secured to the stern timbers. Then the planks could be sprung away from the stern timbers and everything could be examined for damage and deterioration. The planks were all sound and so were the oak stern timbers, but so many fastenings had broken off or eroded in the planks nearest the keel, that Arthur suggested new lengths of planking should be scarfed in and refastened to the ribs and stern timbers to make a really secure job. While the lengths of plank were removed, it was possible to put a long diagonal bolt through all the timbers in the heel to give some rigidity to the area that had taken the brunt of the grounding in the storm.

Incidentally, a newspaper cutting about the storm had the headline "CHAOS AS GALES LEAVE TRAIL OF STORM DAMAGE" and gave details of numerous uprooted trees, broken power lines, missing advertisement hoardings, roofs of some buildings destroyed and ships in distress at sea.

While the planks were removed for replacement, there was some possibility that extreme high tides could flood the boat and submerge the engine, so it was decided that the engine should be lifted out by chain blocks from a strong beam built up after removing the wheelhouse roof and could be dragged back on the cockpit floor, well above any possible flooding. Ron Gray supervised this operation and while the engine was out devised a new way of fitting the engine bolts and strengthening the engine bearers.

I had given up any hopes of boating for the '76 season but Arthur made such good progress that we hoped we might be back afloat by early July and ready for a Summer cruise by a target date of July 24th. This would give us yet one more Summer in Scilly.

In addition to helping Arthur and Ron whenever necessary, I managed to do a rebuild in the galley, replacing the old Taylor paraffin stove with a modern calor gas version, which entailed making a ventilated gas bottle storage space in the cockpit and laying copper piping and flexible armoured piping where necessary. The whole galley was lined with new formica surfaces for easy cleaning and new cupboards with sliding doors for galley cutlery, crockery and cooking utensils. This made a complete transformation, to the joy of all cooking and eating enthusiasts on board.

We did go to sea on target date but everything had been finished in a last minute rush and we were to find a number of irritating minor problems as a result. After leaving the mooring on Sunday July 25th and reaching St Mawes without incident on the Monday, we went on to Scilly on Tuesday, passing Wolf Rock at midday and then began getting engine trouble. Peggy noticed a change in the engine note and found there was no cooling water in the exhaust system and I noticed the engine temperature gauge going sky high. While we wallowed around we went through a procedure we had used before to get rid of an air lock in the engine cooling system. This involved lifting floor boards, turning off a seawater inlet valve, disconnecting a hose and blowing hard through it (head down under the floorboards, a rather sick making procedure at sea) reconnecting it all in the right order, then start the diesel, look over the side and if in luck observe water cooled exhaust again!

We started the old Kelvin wing engine and put up the sails, which was just as well because a few minutes later the same problem reappeared and we were forced to admit the possibility that this was not just a casual airlock, but that we probably had a faulty water circulating pump. This proved indeed to be the case later on. We pressed on slowly for Scilly, making between four and five knots which was quite satisfactory but when we came in through St Mary's Sound, we realized that this rig was no good for beating up against a smart northeasterly breeze and then finding a safe spot to drop the anchor.

The answer was to rig an emergency water supply to the exhaust system consisting of a plastic funnel taped to a length of polythene tube held by one crew member, while crew number two poured sea water into the funnel from a basin, while crew number three kept the water supply going with a bucket on a rope over the side. By using the diesel only at the last moment and keeping it at low revs we achieved the control we needed to come to anchor, but what would anyone ashore with a good pair of binoculars make of this performance going on over the open engine casing by the three busy members of the crew? The system (largely Peggy's inspiration) worked while I did the steering, trying to look unconcerned. We had made St Mary's in ten hours, only an hour over our average time.

The next day, Wednesday, with the help of Ron Gray who had arrived by helicopter for a couple of weeks holiday at Green Farm, the salt water pump was dismantled and a new impeller fitted in the Isles of Scilly Steamship Company's workshop ashore. When refitted we had water cooled exhaust once more but only up to half our normal cruising revs.

Thursday was a day devoted to shrimping with our old friend Derek Pickup and his dog Smokey, but to our dismay on the way back to harbour the cooling water disappeared in a cloud of steam, so our problems were not over yet.

On Friday Ron Gray took the whole exhaust system apart and found that in the extreme heat the inner layer of the exhaust hose had ballooned, causing an almost complete blockage. We were able to cut out the defective part and reconnect the system, hopefully now working perfectly.

The next five days were spent visiting different islands and doing some more shrimping, until on Thursday 5th August we took advantage of a good forecast to run back to the Mainland, enjoying a nine hour run covering the sixty four mile trip to Helford. We spent the next night at St Mawes and then ran up to the river Yealm for our traditional last meal ashore before returning to the Tamar to pick up our mooring on Sunday, ready for Peggy to return to work on Monday.

As I was still enjoying school holidays I took my nephew Andrew Davy for what we called a "Minimate's" cruise from the 16th to the 20th of August. Unfortunately on the run back from Fowey the water cooling problem surfaced again and most of the worrying trip home was with a struggling Kelvin wing engine and several short bursts on the main engine after using the air lock procedure. Once past the breakwater, the main diesel ran faultlessly all the way up the river to the mooring. This provided the clue which finally cured the problem completely. Air had been getting into the seawater intake as the boat rolled, so we put *Fairwater* on the beach and put a new intake much lower down and the problem disappeared for good.

After a few day trips we laid *Fairwater* up on our beach to end the 1976 season which, apart from the engine problems, had been remarkably successful, due to the long spell of dry sunny weather.

Chapter Seven

The usual preparations were made for the '77 season. One satisfying improvement was the replacement of the old cockpit and wheelhouse floorboards with a new set made from greenheart, a virtually indestructible timber so dense that it will not float. Numerous small improvements, refastening and recaulking both garboard planks and the usual antifouling, painting and varnishing ensured that *Fairwater* was fit for sea by early June.

We had a Spring bank holiday cruise from Sunday 5th of June to the 12th. In blustery and rainy conditions we spent most of the week in the beautiful surroundings of the river Yealm. We did get as far as the river Erme to the east and Cawsand to the west and had a happy and relaxed holiday, though we had no cause to be proud of the number of sea miles covered.

We then enjoyed a dozen daytrips in local waters before we embarked on our annual pilgrimage to Scilly.

To make the best use of Peggy's holiday (second and third weeks of August) I took *Fairwater* as far as Falmouth with nephew Andrew Davy for crew in the first week of August and Peggy and Richard Hutchings (godson) arranged to come on board on the evening of Friday August 5th at St Mawes. We all agreed on a day in port on the Saturday because the Queen was visiting St Mawes from the Royal Yacht and visiting yachts were invited to join the locals for a review of yachts to welcome her. We dressed *Fairwater* overall in her smart (home made) signal flags and we had a close view of the Royal Jubilee couple in the Royal Barge at 17:00. We then raised anchor and went across to Helford river entrance to anchor for the night off Durgan. Then we enjoyed a calm sunny evening, with only two other boats in the anchorage. Durgan is an ideal departure point for a voyage to Scilly and Peggy and I got under way at 05:35 next morning, leaving the crew to surface later.

We rounded the Lizard at 07:40, took our departure from the Runnel Stone buoy at 10:42, with 36.4 miles on the log, sighted the Islands at 13:00 and dropped the anchor in St Mary's harbour at 15:00 having covered 65.3 miles.

On Monday 8th August we visited two islands, St Agnes for lunch at the Turk's Head and then across to New Grimsby, Tresco for the night. On Tuesday we visited three islands. St Helen's, back to St Mary's for shopping, then around the Spanish Ledges buoy to the Cove at St Agnes for the night. Wednesday we went around the back of Samson and then landed on Samson Bar to explore the whole island. In the afternoon we returned to St Mary's, anchoring first off Pelistry to drop our passengers (the Gray family) before going back to St Mary's harbour to anchor for the night.

On Thursday we went around the outside of St Martin's and anchored in Porth Morran to explore White Island. We had Derek Pickup on board and we offered to tow back to St Mary's a long plank and a length of 4" x 4" hardwood which we found there, in true Scillonian beachcombing tradition.

Friday was a quiet day in port, where we were delighted to see our friends the Hughes family arrive in *Havssula.*

We travelled with the new arrivals on Saturday to Porth Conger for lunch in the pub, then guided them to New Grimsby where they wanted to spend the night and then we returned to our usual anchorage in St Mary's harbour at 17:00.

On Sunday we went across to Tresco Channel again in the afternoon to take Harry's wife, Syl, for a trip around Round Island, St Helen's Pool, Northwethel, Old Grimsby Channel, inside the Kettle and back to New Grimsby. We anchored close to *Havssula* for tea and then went back to St Mary's once more.

Monday was a 'Vintage Scillonian Day', high pressure, calm hazy sunshine, a few fog patches and a very successful shrimping expedition, anchoring between Hedge Rock and Tean, catching about two gallons before lunchtime. We then spent the night anchored off Old Grimsby.

The fine Summer weather broke on Tuesday with near gale force winds and heavy drizzling rain so we had a rough passage back to the anchorage at St Mary's, where we had invited Derek Pickup and his wife on board for an evening meal. By the time they came on board the rain had stopped and the sun came out, but strong winds made choppy conditions in the harbour, with *Fairwater* pitching gently in the sparkling waves. Our guests were not put off by the exhilarating conditions and Peggy produced a superb Tresco mullet in cider and fennel, with a generous prawn sauce. Good food, good wine, good company made this a memorable evening.

The next day we left St Mary's for the seclusion of the Cove on St Agnes. The boys went fishing in the dinghy (four pollack, three mackerel) but deteriorating weather sent us back to St Mary's in a strong northeast breeze with heavy patches of drizzle. St Mary's harbour is well sheltered from the northeast but the Cove is not. After spending the next day quietly in port, we headed up channel on Friday for St Mawes, then St Mawes to the river Yealm for the traditional visit to the Old Ship at Newton Ferrers.

Back on the mooring on Sunday, having altogether covered 486 miles. I have listed our movements around the Scillies in some detail at the risk of becoming boring, to show the frenetic way we tried to see as much of the Islands as possible once we arrived there.

The usual day trips ended the season; down river to the Sound or up river to St Germans or Calstock. As always the process of laying the boat up for the Winter was accompanied by dreams of taking her back to the Isles of Scilly for the next Summer's cruise.

Chapter Eight

Christmas '77 saw the completion of the workshop on our quay, now twenty one feet by ten feet, raised on nine inch thick pitch pine beams over what used to be the workshop, but in future would be simply a store for boat's gear. It was wired with plenty of power sockets and lockable steel cabinets stored the tools and made the base for one of the benches. The two main Winter jobs on *Fairwater* were the removal of the main prop shaft and coupling, the whole lot being sent to a specialist engineering firm at Southampton for expert attention and secondly the installation of what was to prove a great boon for Scillonian cruising, a powerful electric anchor winch.

By now we had such confidence in *Fairwater* that Peggy and I decided we would try a one week cruise for the Spring bank holiday on our own. On Sunday May 28th we pottered down channel and anchored off Portloe for lunch in The Lugger and thence on to St Mawes by 17:30. Monday was a lazy day in one hundred per cent sunshine, watching the sailing activity around us, taking an afternoon trip up the Fal and then returning to St Mawes for the night after enjoying a meal ashore. On Tuesday we took a friend across to Helford village for lunch at the Shipwright's Arms. On Wednesday we moved back up channel to Fowey and on Friday to the river Yealm to ensure our traditional end of cruise meal ashore at the Old Ship. Having returned to our mooring on Sunday, we felt that all the effort and expense of rebuilding *Fairwater* was justified when she could give us the pleasure of cruising when and where we chose in comfort.

A week after our return we put *Fairwater* in on our beach to give the old Kelvin paraffin wing engine a thorough refit. Ron Gray did a typically meticulous job, taking the engine apart, regrinding valves, renewing studs and giving the product a trial run on Tuesday 20th June. Although the engine started readily enough, Ron found at the end of the run that cooling water was finding its way through the block into the cylinders. This major problem, added to the impossibility of obtaining spares had only one solution. The old Kelvin should be laid to rest (now nearly forty years old) and replaced with a new diesel. But was there a diesel that would fit in the very shallow space on the port side and line up with the existing propeller shaft and stern gland? If such an engine existed, was there time (just over four weeks) to find one and fit it before our Summer holiday. Volvos, Yammars and Petters were briefly considered, but the hand of Providence led us to the Cornish Arms at Gunnislake for an evening meal on Thursday and we found the answer in the form of Mike Challis, the local Sabb dealer. He told us that these Norwegian built diesels were still constructed on traditional, ultra reliable lines and that the 10HP single cylinder version had, in his experience, replaced Kelvins in the past. Yes, he could show us one the next day and Ron and I inspected one at the works, which Ron only faulted because of the vibration inherent in any single cylinder engine. Armed with leaflets and spurred on by the knowledge that Mike Challis could get us an engine quickly if we could give him the order by Sunday, we decided that the perfect answer would be the larger 2 cylinder 18Hp Sabb, if it would fit. If our calculations were wrong we would have a very expensive disaster on our hands, but if things worked out, *Fairwater* would be transformed into an even more powerful T.S.D.Y (Twin Screw Diesel Yacht) with extra safety in the event of main engine failure, easy starting compared with the old Kelvin and vastly improved electrical system on board with a second alternator to call on.

From the leaflet I was able to produce an accurate full size plywood template of the Sabb, the old Kelvin was dismantled and removed and the template installed in its place. We found it fitted with less than an inch of length to spare, three sixteenths of an inch had to be chopped out of the stringer to clear the coupling and when installed, there would be only a few millimetres clearance between the alternator of the Sabb and the header tank of the main engine cooling system. As the Duke of Wellington said about Waterloo: "A damned near run thing".

Our friend Harry Hughes was brought in to check our calculations, being a highly skilled precision and aircraft engineer and a very experienced yachtsman as well. He gave us the 'thumbs up' and after hectic discussions on the installation equipment, we were able to place our order with Mike Challis, as requested, on the Sunday evening. The gleaming new engine was delivered to our garage the following Wednesday!

Once again *Fairwater* was weaving her spell to entrap a team of devotees to achieve magic results. Our shipwright friend Arthur Keith undertook the installation of the new engine beds with me helping with the woodwork; Ron improvised a new rubber cutless bearing for the Kelvin's old 'A' bracket and adapted the old shaft log to take the new Sabb inboard bearing in spite of the difficulties caused by having to replace the old one inch bronze propeller shaft with the new twenty five millimetre stainless steel one. A new bank of heavy duty 12 volt batteries was added, for which Phil made new fittings, to supply the new anchor winch.

By the 4th July the new engine beds were in and the engine was lowered on to them from Saltash quay on Friday 7th (having taken off the wheelhouse roof) and on the Saturday and Sunday following we installed the flexible exhaust hose, silencer, fuel supply, fuel filter and sea water cooling inlet ready for lining up.

By Monday 10th, Phil and his friend Geoff completed the new electric wiring and the engine started for the first time. We were unable to do sea trials as we were 'neaped' on the beach and then on the 13th the new electric anchor winch at last arrived so we remained on the beach while the old Moyle winch was removed and the new one installed in its place. The electrics were completed by Phil and Geoff on Monday, a new 180' anchor chain brought home from Simpson Lawrence on Tuesday, engine trials Wednesday, fuelling up and putting stores on board on Thursday and crew arrived on board ready for our Summer cruise on Friday 21st.

PHEW !

We made the usual earliest possible start, leaving the mooring at 18:15, barely an hour after Peggy arrived home from work. We had our nephew Andrew Davy and Richard Hutchings on board as crew. We were content to spend the night at anchor off Cawsand and awoke next morning to overcast skies and freshening southwest wind. Any gloom caused by this was dispelled by the sheer joy of raising anchor with the new electric winch. The headwind and choppy conditions off Penlee Point and Rame Head required reduced speed to prevent too much slamming and spray, so we used the main engine only, resisting the temptation to put the new Sabb on as well until midday when we reached rather more sheltered conditions. We spent the night in Wiseman's Pool upstream from Fowey in a deluge of rain, followed by another deluge of rain for most of the next day. The crew settled into reading, playing cards, struggling to get some sort of reception on the television, eating crisps etcetera until the weather cleared enough in the evening for the crew to have a run ashore at Fowey while the skipper was left on watch.

On Monday July 24th we moved on to the Helford river to anchor off the village and we left there at 07:30 next morning in spite of the forecast of southwest winds force two to three becoming westerly force four to five later. We should have had more patience and waited in the perfect shelter of Helford to see what the weather was going to do. As it was we had a rough ride around the Lizard, followed by menacing looking skies, a dropping barometer and a southwest wind now up to force five. We headed inshore towards Penzance for shelter and reluctantly went into Newlyn harbour, knowing it to be an overcrowded commercial fishing port. Nevertheless we were greeted cheerfully by the Harbourmaster and decided to tie up beside half a dozen fishing boats, eventually finding ourselves the middle boat of thirteen fishing boats, all driven in by the bad weather.

Peggy and the boys went ashore next morning to find the Harbourmaster and pay our harbour dues. The next pleasant surprise was to find that for 49 pence we could stay as long as we wished!

Wednesday and Wednesday night were very wet and windy, with dreadful creaking and squealing noises from the fenders of boats alongside as they strained to and fro. We were lucky enough to be offered a large crayfish that had just shed its shell and was therefore not marketable, for £7.00 instead of £20.00 by one of the fishermen. We dined on it like lords for two days.

The weather cleared on Friday after a monumental downpour on Thursday, so we left Newlyn harbour after a most interesting stay and headed for Scilly where we arrived at 14:00. On Saturday, after taking on some water from the quay we went to the Cove at St Agnes for the night, catching 15 mackerel on the way over.

Richard's mother, father and brother had arrived for a self catering holiday in a cottage at Lunnon and we picked them up from the quay for a trip on Sunday morning, when Peggy enlivened the proceedings by falling overboard as we manoeuvred into the steps. As she dried and changed down below we headed across to Tresco Channel, past Cromwell's Castle and around Round Island in some pretty rough conditions before finding a sheltered spot to anchor for tea in St Helen's Pool. As the wind was by now about force five northwesterly, St Mary's Harbour would be uncomfortably rough so we took our guests to Porthcressa which was very crowded, but we found a spot close in to the beach where we ferried our passengers ashore.

On Monday we took our friends Roger and Alba Williams across to the Cove, St Agnes in spite of strong westerly winds and by the time we returned to Porthcressa in the late afternoon the wind had strengthened and the weather was so overcast and threatening that we laid out a kedge anchor to avoid dragging back among the 40 or so other boats astern of us in the anchorage. Overnight the wind rose to gale force, with heavy rain, but our two anchors held securely and close in to the shelter of the beach *Fairwater* lay still and cosy in spite of the wind shrieking through the rigging.

Next morning it was still blowing about force six but clearing skies brought sunshine enough to encourage us to take the Hutchings family across to the Cove again at St Agnes, where we lunched happily in the Turk's Head. I then made the excuse to be on 'anchor watch' on board while everyone else did the tour of St Agnes on foot. Eventually we returned to our spot in the anchorage at Porthcressa about teatime.

On Wednesday, with our old friend Derek Pickup on board, we cruised around St Mary's from Peninnis to Toll's Island at slow speed while the lads caught 30 mackerel and then threaded our way through the Eastern Islands before returning to St Mary's. The Islands were looking even more beautiful than usual but the crew were sad at the prospect of our imminent departure for the Mainland after what seemed a very short visit.

Next day we returned to St Mawes, reaching Fowey on Friday and the river Yealm on Saturday for the traditional end of cruise celebration. Several day trips brought the season to an end and little was done on *Fairwater* in the stormy Winter of '78/'79, as stone wall building and a greenhouse project kept me busy in the garden, while the boat sat safely on the beach below.

Chapter Nine

1979

Probably as a result of my neglect of *Fairwater* during the Winter, she had her own back on me when, after the usual fitting out, we were going out to pick up the mooring buoy when the Commodore engine came to a halt with a cloud of grey smoke flying from the exhaust. Ron Gray was called in with some urgency to find that water in the fuel tanks had done the damage and the boat had to stay put while fuel pump, injectors and fuel supply were put right. As this took some time, we had the opportunity to improve some of the ship's electrics, engine installation and gas supply to the galley. Eventually all improvements worked well and *Fairwater* was given some running trials in the river and was all ready for her Summer cruise by Sunday 15th July.

As we only had five days in Scilly last year, we decided that I would take *Fairwater* down there nearly two weeks ahead of Peggy's holiday, with the same two lads as crew as last year, while Peggy could fly down from Plymouth to Scilly as soon as her holiday started and enjoy the maximum amount of time there.

We actually left the mooring on Sunday 22nd July at 17:55 and only went as far as Cawsand, which was calm and sheltered from the gentle northwest wind. This was ideal for us to settle down to life on board and after our evening meal the lads rowed ashore before returning for a good night's undisturbed sleep.

Next morning they were roused from their bunks soon after I heard the shipping forecast at 05:55, because although the winds were only forecast satisfactorily as force three to four northwesterly, there was a mention of rain or fog later, so it would pay us to make an early start. Having breakfasted well, we raised anchor at Cawsand at 07:45, hoping to make Falmouth. However, by 09:30 when we were off Polperro visibility started closing in as forecast and the cliffs leading on to Fowey disappeared completely in a bank of fog, leaving only a ribbon of white breaking on the rocks around the base of the cliffs visible. As we had to slow down to three knots in the fog we thought we might as well take advantage of the situation and put the mackerel lines out as we headed for the entrance to Fowey. Having landed the ideal number for our requirements, six, we took the lines in to save any possible complications if we had to manoeuvre to avoid a collision with another vessel, found the Fowey entrance and anchored above Polruan at noon.

We were just resigning ourselves to making the most of our rather short trip down channel with a night's stay surrounded by the delights of Fowey harbour when the fog began to lift and as the Harbourmaster had not yet collected our harbour dues for the night, we made a rapid departure for Falmouth at 14:40, in good visibility and anchored eventually off St Mawes at 18:30, having covered just over 44 miles.

The fog and patches of drizzle returned next morning, but in spite of this, after shopping ashore, we headed across the bay to Helford village and had pasties for lunch at the Shipwright's Arms, to the huge delight of the crew. In the afternoon, as the weather cleared, the lads went fishing in the dinghy and came back with a good sized bass caught on a mackerel spinner!

Wednesday's early morning shipping forecast remained the same westerly force three to four becoming southerly force three, fog patches and rain later. Such was the call of the Islands we decided to move down channel and risk having to navigate in fog. A thick patch descended on us just as we passed the Manacles buoy and as I didn't fancy navigating 'blind' around the Lizard, we found our way into Coverack, which we had not visited before and anchored there at 09:00, hoping the fog would clear.

The boys rowed ashore for some shopping and as the fog lifted we left for the Lizard at 10:15. Visibility was still poor as we crossed Mounts Bay but with calm conditions, I decided we would spend the night at anchor off Mousehole, giving ourselves the best possible departure point for a crossing to Scilly next day. We had a pleasant visit ashore to that most delightful Cornish fishing village in the evening and as the fog became so dense that we could not see the harbour wall on one side, or St Clement's Isle on the other, we put our electric anchor light up the forestay and spent the night in the eerie atmosphere of our own little circle of floodlit fog.

We woke to greet a calm sunny morning with all the fog miraculously disappeared. We raised anchor in good spirits and with the prospect of a long sunny day ahead, we decided to do the crossing to Scilly, under the power of our shiny new Sabb diesel, to help its running in programme and it drove us smoothly there in five hours, at just under six knots. Its quiet soothing engine note was much more pleasant than the powerful, raucous noise of the main BMC Commodore diesel. We completed the 36 mile journey to St Mary's harbour by 14:20 hours.

We spent the next seven days travelling around the Islands, enjoying nights at anchor in the Cove, St Agnes, Tresco Channel, Watermill Cove, St Mary's and, most frequently, in our favourite spot near the Lifeboat Slip in St Mary's harbour.

Friday 3rd August was an important day because the boat had to be prepared for 'Admiral's Inspection' by Peggy as she was due to arrive on the Brymon flight from Plymouth. We were anchored in Porthcressa where we were sheltered from the northwest wind and Derek Pickup drove me up to the airport with, sadly, a very ill Smokey, the cocker Spaniel who had accompanied us on numerous walks and boat trips around the Islands. He managed a few enthusiastic tail wags to welcome Peggy, but he died just a few days later. It was a lovely sunny day on which to welcome the 'chief cook and bottle washer' back on board and after enjoying a beautiful flight over the length of the Cornish coast on an almost empty Otter aircraft, we were all happy that Peggy could start her fortnight's holiday on board, down in the Scillies.

After a quick shopping expedition ashore, we were off on our voyaging again as soon as possible, leaving Porthcressa at 10:20, to catch five mackerel off Peninnis before heading across to St Agnes to anchor in the Cove for the night, to the delight of all the crew.

Over the next four days we visited Old Grimsby, St Mary's again and Tresco Channel where we were able to help some newly made friends in a 27' *Finnsailer* by lending them a spare anchor when a gale blew up overnight on Thursday.

After the gale cleared, we moved about the Islands, shrimping and taking friends out for trips, just the usual routine, until the evening of Monday 13th August when we watched the evening weather forecast on the television while the evening meal was cooking.

There was another southwesterly gale force eight on the way, but it was described as "intensifying" and "moving rapidly" and there was something about the facial expression of the forecaster that was full of foreboding. St Mary's harbour was calm but an ominous greenish haze covered the sky and I made the unpopular decision (because the evening meal would have to be delayed) that we would raise anchor and leave the harbour, where the anchorage would be exposed to the oncoming gale, which would inevitably go west and then northwest as it passed through. We went across to Tresco Channel where we would be briefly exposed to the southwesterly as the bad weather came in but where the high hills of Bryher would shelter us as the winds changed.

This gale proved to be the notorious storm which overwhelmed the fleet of yachts in the Fastnet race, costing much loss of life and damage to the yachts. As I anticipated, St Mary's harbour became a disaster area with boats dragging anchors and huge seas broke over the quay to swamp the boats that tied up beside it for shelter. We heard the sudden shift from southwest to northwest that caused the damage, but apart from the shrieking of the wind through our rigging, that shift put us in the lee of Bryher and *Fairwater* ceased leaping about and lay still for the rest of the night.

Next morning Radio Cornwall described the havoc and we listened in to *Fairwater's* radio telephone which we could not use to transmit news of our safety because all channels were devoted to the rescue operation.

Eventually we managed to get ashore in the dinghy to telephone our good news from the telephone box on Bryher. As darkness fell we watched St Mary's lifeboat head out through Tresco Channel into the strong seas yet again to tow another damaged survivor in. The lifeboat crew had been out all night and all day without rest or hot food and they deserved the cheers and applause given them by the boats sheltering in Tresco Channel close to us as they returned.

As our holiday time was running out we decided to head for home in spite of the leftover heavy swells from the gale. At least they ran in the right direction to help us home. We left Tresco Channel at 07:40 and anchored in the Helford river at 18:00, having kept company around the Lizard with a returning Fastnet racer which was travelling on engine only, with her mast and rigging all gone.

Thursday 16th August's weather forecast proved we had chosen the right day to run home. A southwesterly force nine with heavy rain was on the way. We dodged the gale in the Helford estuary, spending some time at Port Navas Creek where we met up with the Osman family, with whom we had made friends in Scilly. We retrieved a large kedge anchor from them which they had needed to borrow to ride out the strong weather and we enjoyed their hospitality with a barbecue party in the evening, when the youngsters swam in their floodlit swimming pool, in the rain!

Next day, Saturday, was Port Navas Regatta and we dressed *Fairwater* overall in honour of the occasion. We left it as late as we could to run up channel towards home and left Helford entrance, with our friends waving us goodbye from the boat *Faroyar*, in Helford entrance.

After going through very choppy conditions off Falmouth we passed the Dodman close to, at 19:00 and picked up a mooring in Wiseman's Pool at Fowey at 21:00. Sunday was a quiet but drizzly day and after catching 32 mackerel off Rame Head we returned to our home mooring at 14:45.

A dozen day trips, some down river to Cawsand, or fishing off Rame Head and some up river to Calstock or Weir Head completed a very satisfactory season.

Chapter Ten

1980
The Year of the Dogs

In February we acquired Skip, our beautiful liver and white Springer Spaniel and a few weeks later we added Ike, the black and white puppy still unsold from the same litter, a quiet, loving dog, to complete our crew. They were both introduced to *Fairwater* and the noise of her diesel engines when still young puppies and they were easily persuaded to enjoy the experience as much as their owners.

For the first time since 1973 Andrew Davy, our nephew, was not able to join us as his school days were now behind him and he was in France, learning the skills of producing French charcuterie. We had brothers Andrew and Richard Hutchings instead and as before, they were used as crew to take *Fairwater* to Scilly where my wife could join us a couple of weeks later.

Having left home on Saturday, 26th July, we spent the next six days in the St Mawes and Helford area, waiting for a break in the wet and windy weather which would allow us a crossing to Scilly. This we finally achieved on Friday August 1st, after some hesitation because of a shipping forecast of a gale warning for Sole. I woke up the very sleepy crew of two boys and two dogs at 04:00 and headed out into Falmouth Bay by moonlight in order to catch a favourable tide around the Lizard. The more up to date forecast at 06:25 gave variable winds becoming southerly force four, so we had our confidence restored for our voyage to the Isles. By the time we were anchored in St Mary's harbour at 16:00 and went ashore for a dog walk the crew began to recover rapidly from the stresses and strains of the long day at sea; twelve hours of it!

The next six days provided the usual diet of gales and near gale force winds, which only dropped to a force four once, while we dodged around from St Mary's harbour to Watermill and to Tresco Channel to try to find shelter. Typical August monsoon!

Peggy arrived by Brymon flight from Plymouth midday on Thursday 7th August to the unashamed delight of both two legged and four legged crew, who relished the prospect of better food than that provided by the skipper.

With Peggy on board we immediately returned to our island hopping routine, anchoring in Tresco Channel for the night. Next morning we headed back to St Mary's to catch a dozen mackerel off Peninnis before going to St Agnes to anchor in the Cove. Blue sky and sunshine greeted our arrival there, to the delight of Peggy, whose favourite anchorage this was, but to the chagrin of Andrew who was due to catch the Scillonian back to the Mainland next day.

To make sure he caught the boat we did not stay at St Agnes overnight but headed back to St Mary's in a flat calm. Having seen Andrew depart, we took a friend on a trip around the Eastern Islands, catching a couple of dozen mackerel in the process before returning to the harbour to dine on fish pie.

Wet and windy weather returned for the next five days but we still moved around the Islands; the dogs always had a run ashore before breakfast, with the skipper, regardless of weather, with their joy and enthusiasm for a runaround on the land always making up for the misery of the weather.

Friday 15th August provided a solitary pleasant sunny day before the usual gale warnings for Sole returned on Saturday, with promises of rain and fog. In spite of this we made a bad weather crossing to Porth Conger on St Agnes, walking around the island in wet and windy conditions before returning to St Mary's harbour for a night of fog and drizzle with the wind moderating to a southwesterly three to four.

On Sunday we visited St Helen's Pool, Old Grimsby anchorage and finally ended up in Tresco Channel after an exciting trip around the Kettle, provided by the steep Atlantic swell off Shipman Head.

Having returned the next day to Porthcressa, St Mary's, we were encouraged by a reasonable shipping forecast to head back up channel next day, which we did in nine hours, enjoying a rare calm and gentle rounding of the Lizard before anchoring in the Helford. This visit to our much loved Falmouth area was made even more enjoyable than usual by the arrival of *Havssula* with our friends the Hughes on board with their two dogs. We travelled in company to Port Navas, St Mawes and Trelissick with much socialising and dog walking.

On Friday we moved on from Falmouth to Fowey, taking advantage of the gentle offshore breeze to anchor off Portloe for lunch ashore at the Lugger where we were given a friendly welcome by the management and provided with a table on the terrace which suited dogs as well. Next day, back to the mooring on the Tamar, having covered 382 miles and proved that both doggy and human crew could enjoy a cruise to Scilly in unfavourable weather conditions.

The Winter period 1980/1981 was made interesting by being able to store *Fairwater's* gear in our own facilities on our quay for the first time and by the fact that we decided to replace our old and heavy Commodore diesel with a lighter, quieter Volvo engine, similar in design to the Sabb which we were so pleased with. As usual the removal of the old engine and the installation of the new one was to be a D.I.Y job using our own facilities. The only exception to this principle had to be the use of a crane capable of lifting out the heavy old engine. The only one we could find at the sort of price we wanted to pay was an old hand crane vintage 1860 at the rear of Fox and Haggart's engineering works on the Barbican at Plymouth.

We had by now found a buyer for the old engine who was pleased to pay £450.00 for it, which pleased us as that was as much as we had paid for it in the first place. The new owner agreed to transport it away from the Barbican, while we agreed to bring *Fairwater* down on a suitable weekend in early December and crane the engine out. All went well, in spite of the difficult logistics of getting everything together at precisely the right time on a weekend when the engineering works would be closed. The shiny new Volvo arrived to be stored in our garage while necessary measurements were made over the Christmas holiday period; this holiday being pleasantly complicated by our silver wedding anniversary celebrations on Boxing Day.

New engine beds, stern tube, inboard and outboard bearings were all installed before our return visit to the crane in the Barbican on 7th February to lift the new engine off a trailer and lower it into its hopefully correct position on board.

Fairwater's trip down river to the Barbican and back was a cause for concern because she could only be powered by the Sabb wing engine, which was useless for manoeuvring as there was no rudder behind it to steer with. We had to be prepared to use a dinghy with an outboard as 'tug' to position her, until she could be driven forward at sufficient speed for the rudder to take control. All went well, thanks to the favourable weather conditions and the wheelhouse roof was rebuilt as we came up river to ensure that our new £3,000's worth of engine would be snug and dry.

It took until Whitsun to complete the installation work, plus the usual refitting and improvements and the installation of a Nautech 3000 autopilot which was to make the navigation of *Fairwater* a much easier and more precise operation than it had ever been before. At this stage it was cause for great satisfaction to think that our 'old wreck' was now largely rebuilt, re-engined and fitted with new furniture and navigation equipment to a standard that would be hard to find on a new G.R.P. vessel without laying out a huge sum of money.

Chapter Eleven

For the Spring bank holiday cruise from the 23rd May to the 29th May, 1981, we were limited by poor weather conditions to the coast between the river Yealm and the river Fowey. This limited cruising area proved satisfactory from two points of view: firstly we were able to give the new Volvo main engine a good few hours running in time, without straying too far from base in case any problems cropped up with the new installation. Secondly, our young and enthusiastic doggy crew guided us to many of their favourite walks without having to spend too many hours of (to them) boring passage making at sea, where they were deprived of their normal navigational aids of the smell of various trees, bushes and patches of grass.

This was all good training for the much more serious job, a month later, of crewing *Fairwater* down to the Isles of Scilly, where Peggy would join us after flying down from Plymouth.

Having made use of the intervening weeks to prepare *Fairwater* for sea, when we actually came to leave the mooring on the morning of Saturday 25th July, we found the all important main batteries connected to the Sabb diesel inexplicably flat. This not only made it impossible to start the engine, but we could not use the anchor winch or many other supplies to lights, radio and navigational equipment on board.

As always a panic call to the faithful Phil Robins brought the necessary jump leads with which to start the engine and to begin to generate some electricity. Then his patient expertise found that a faulty bilge pump had switched itself on and then failed to switch off, thus draining the batteries completely. This fault was eradicated and in the time remaining to us we were able to make Fowey that evening and then spend Sunday crossing St Austell Bay to Portmellon for lunch, then on to St Mawes for the night, using the Sabb engine as much as possible to boost the still very low batteries. Part of the running was made on the Sabb engine alone, trailing a couple of mackerel spinners, which provided us with eight fish in the bucket by the time we arrived. Mackerel is much appreciated by Skip and Ike as well as the human crew, although they prefer theirs pressure cooked into a paste so no bones can scratch their throats.

The next day we went across to Helford, just nicely timed for crew and dogs to enjoy lunch in the Shipwright's Arms. A dinghy trip to Port Navas to see some friends occupied the afternoon and the evening passed quickly with cooking, eating and phoning home and planning the trip to Scilly for the next day to make the best use of the tides; should the weather forecast be favourable.

On Tuesday 28th July we made our crossing to the Isles of Scilly. We raised anchor at 07:00 after hearing the early morning shipping forecast, breakfasting and dog walking. It was flat calm but there was a fog bank shrouding the Helford river entrance, which was no surprise as we heard the St Anthony lighthouse foghorn sounding through most of the night. We had some anxious minutes trying to find the Manacles buoy to ensure that we did not end up on the Manacles rocks, but it did eventually turn up right under our noses in a clear patch, gradually extending towards the Lizard, which we passed in good visibility before enjoying a calm sunny trip across Mounts Bay, passing Penzance at 10:35.

So far, so good, but at the Runnel Stone buoy near Land's End, fog banks could be seen ahead, so we turned in towards the beach at Porthcurnow and anchored close inshore, in beautiful sunshine. Crowds of holidaymakers were enjoying the sand and the sea, happily unaware of the anxiety of the crew on the *Fairwater*, who were faced with worry. I was responsible for the life of my one teenage crew and my loyal Springers. Should I risk a passage to the Islands in fog, without the benefit of accurate navigational equipment, such as the Decca we were to install later? Should we turn back in such calm and sunny conditions to find an anchorage near Penzance, where yet more fog could cause problems?

What I decided was to send young Philip ashore in the dinghy, with the dogs, at least they would appreciate the midvoyage break, to find a telephone box and ask St Mary's Coastguard for a visibility report. They said there was a mile and a half visibility but there were fog patches around. At least the Islands were not completely fogbound. So we enjoyed a quiet sandwich lunch and as no fog bank closed in on us, we got underway again, making an accurate departure from the Runnel Stone buoy at 13:00 with 34.3 miles on the log. We then let the faithful autopilot steer us accurately, while we kept watch.

Two hours later, just over half way across to the Islands, we ran into thick fog, which remained with us for the rest of the trip. When our distance run began to approach 59 (this being a check on our ETA) we dispensed with the Sabb engine and gently cruised on with the Volvo only, giving us much better manoeuvrability to make an emergency stop.

We were very relieved at 16:25, when a few seconds of a clear patch in the fog revealed water breaking at the foot of the very distinctive outline of the island of Hanjague, which stands out to sea off the Eastern Islands. From there it was no great problem to find the entrance to Crow Sound, then to St Mary's itself and finally an anchorage in the fogbound harbour.

Wednesday the 29th was nominated as a quiet day in port to recover from the stress of the passage. Anyway, it was Royal Wedding day for Prince Charles and Princess Diana and the T.V. reception in the harbour is usually good. We dressed *Fairwater* in her flags overall in honour of the occasion, the only other vessel to do the same being the new Scillies RNLI Lifeboat. Blue sky all day, with *Fairwater* sheltered from the northeasterly force 4, gave a memorable day to all on board, not least Philip and the dogs who enjoyed numerous dogwalks ashore, contrasting with the anxious day spent at sea the day before.

Thursday proved to be a typical perfect Scillonian day. Sunshine, dogwalk, shopping, fishing off the Spanish Ledges buoy (eleven mackerel), anchoring in Porth Conger, St Agnes, right under the windows of the Turk's Head for lunch ashore. Then across to New Grimsby harbour, Tresco, to anchor for the night sheltered from the force 5 easterly wind.

Overnight a change of wind direction altered conditions completely as so often happens in the Islands. The wind went north and we rolled miserably in the swell and the tide coming into Tresco Channel from the open Atlantic around Shipman Head. Philip was nearly rolled out of his bunk in the fo'c'sle and in fact his watch did fall to the floor and smash its glass. Skip and Ike, curled up together on their blanket in the cabin doorway slept blissfully through it all as usual.

Worse was to come next morning, when we all went ashore for a walk on Bryher to enjoy the feel of '*terra firma*' underfoot. The weather did another complete change about during a brief spell of thundery rain. This not only cut short the dog walking, but to our horror the now onshore wind had pushed *Fairwater* on to the rocky shore of Tresco, on a dropping tide, making her bounce and judder on the granite boulders as we scrambled on board from the dinghy, to drive her out on main engine and anchor winch before she became a wreck.

We spent the rest of the day at anchor in deeper water, anxiously watching for any sign of leakage. What we did not find until the end of the season was that we had damaged the deadwood aft of the iron keel and a few more bumps could have destroyed our rudder bearing. Yet again the wind went northerly overnight, giving us some restless hours of rock and roll.

With typical Scillonian contrast, the next day, Saturday 1st of August, was all sunshine, relaxation and enjoyment. We left Tresco Channel at 09:00, fished for mackerel off Peninnis, St Mary's, anchored in Porthcressa for shopping and lunch ashore, leaving again at 14:15 for the Cove, St Agnes, to enjoy that most beautiful of all Scillonian anchorages for the night.

We awoke to 100% sunshine and flat calm in the Cove, with the terns wheeling against pure blue sky and diving over the silvery shoals of sand els clearly visible in the transparent water. We enjoyed this unbelievably beautiful day until teatime, when we headed back to St Mary's harbour, to arrange with Derek Pickup yet another traditional Scillonian delight, a day's shrimping in Tresco Channel.

With the help of Derek's shrimp nets and in spite of the frantic attempts of the dogs to help by beating the shrimps to death with their front paws as they swam around us in circles, we caught half a bucket full, about a gallon, which we cooked on board after lunch, some going ashore with Derek to be put in the deep freeze to await Peggy's arrival and two huge helpings were peeled for prawn salads for the evening meal. (N.B. prawns are called 'shrimps' by the Scillonians and they should know, because the pure waters of the Atlantic flowing over the sandbanks and the lush clumps of seaweed produce the most beautifully flavoured 'shrimps' imaginable.)

The next day, Tuesday, was spent in St Mary's harbour because it was the day on which Philip Newton had to be put on *Scillonian III* for a sad departure back to the Mainland. While waiting on board, waiting interminably for departure time, Ike added to the gloom by putting his head skywards and howling in utter misery! What a sad, sensitive, lovely dog he is!

For the next three days, before Peggy's arrival, I had the pleasure of the company of Paul, the teenage son of our good friends Roger and Alba Williams who live on the Islands.

Saturday, 8th August, was the day when Peggy arrived from Plymouth by air. For the next two weeks we enjoyed better than average weather and we cruised amongst and around the Islands, fishing, shrimping and taking friends out for day trips, with very few days anchored in the harbour. Skip and Ike loved every day. Dinghy trips ashore before breakfast when they perched with their forepaws gripping the gunwale to watch the bow wave sweep past, to be followed by the ecstatic walk ashore to enjoy all the familiar sights and smells and, always discreetly and cleaned up afterwards, to do what a dog has got to do after a night on a boat.

So many islands to visit; so many friends to take with us. So many picnic lunches on board and so many pub lunches when we could arrange it. No mechanical problems, no storms. This must have been our best Scillonian holiday ever.

Summer of '81

Don't mourn for the Summer as Autumn commences,
Rich treasures live on, locked up in our senses,
Loud outboards sing, then only silence is heard,
Or soft surf on sand, or the cry of a bird.

Sea emerald and sapphire edged with silver and gold,
Green islands and black rocks our eyes still behold.
Shrimp nets push through brown weed, brown faces smile in the sun,
Happy people crowd the pubs when the long day is done.

And scents fill our senses, strong fennel and samphire
And smoke from tobacco and smoke from a bonfire.
Salt winds from the ocean, salt weed on the sand,
And the bouquet of Summer from the glass in your hand.

Taste fresh shrimps and fresh fish and moules marinière,
Warm red wine on the beaches with love in the air.
And the smell of fair hair and the taste of a kiss,
The flavour of Heaven must be just like this.

The fifth sense of feeling, with joy ever fleeting,
Brings happiness too with the chance of a meeting.
And sorrow that's shared, and the meeting of minds,
The quiet companionship one so rarely finds.

Don't plan for tomorrow, don't sigh for the past,
When things are so good they just simply can't last.
Whatever life brings we must greet it with smiles,
In the Heaven on Earth; the most Fortunate Isles.

We finally returned to the Mainland on Friday August 21st, to anchor fo the night at St Mawes. Having helped us navigate accurately back, ou Nautech autopilot ceased to function off the mouth of the Helford river, bu we managed the easy coastal navigation back to the Yealm on Saturday without its help, for our traditional end of cruise meal ashore with the dogs

So then back to the mooring on the Tamar, Sunday August 23rd. Th ship's log told us that we had covered 400 miles at sea. This may not soun a lot but if you average it out at between six and seven miles per hour, i represents quite a number of hours travelling at sea.

Once safely back on the mooring, we gave *Fairwater* very little use fo the rest of the season, because I was busy removing an ash tree and rebuilding the terrace it was trying to destroy at home. When we finally brough *Fairwater* to our beach, for what I hoped would be a routine Winter layu and Spring fitting out, she seemed to take an age to come over the mud o the rising tide and after securing her on the beach for the night, the followin day revealed a problem so serious that it called into question whether th repair work could be justified for 'just one more summer' in the Scillies.

We found that the wooden deadwood aft of the iron ballast keel wa hanging down several inches at its forward end, with a piece of tough ol branch jammed in it, explaining the boat's reluctance to come in over the mud. This must have been the result of our grounding on Tresco on the 31st of August and how we had travelled so many miles since, in this damaged condition, with the dislodged timber supporting the bearing for the rudder is almost unbelievable.

Common sense dictates that with so much work to do on the house, the garden and the workshop on the quay, that now would be a good time to do a quick repair job and sell the old boat cheaply just to remove the millstone of finance and labour that *Fairwater* hangs about my neck. What she cost us in maintenance and repair each year would pay for a Summer holiday in one of the best hotels in Scilly anyway. Or on some island in the Mediterranean for a change.

But there she sits on the beach with her wooden keel falling off, looking old and worn and tired after a Summer's hard cruising. What hotel can take you around the Cornish coast and the Islands like this lovely old triumph of the shipwright's art? What would the dogs think of being put in kennels while my wife and I disappear into the sea of grey haired guests in some boring hotel? Get on with it John. Get her in on the grid and get her jacked up and bring in a real shipwright to do justice to the vital repair work necessary. I stand on the beach and talk to her. She says "Didn't I look after you for weeks at sea, after that crippling damage that I kept secretly to myself?" Then she says "Isn't it time that you now should look after me?"

As always when help was needed, our ideal shipwright appeared, Paul Dunbar, with whom Peggy had come into contact in the course of her work with Sun Alliance Insurance. Paul was a surveyor, with a background of working on wooden fishing boats, with a wide range of skills and a dogged determination to repair and restore any worthwhile wooden boat he could lay his hands on. Thanks to his initiative and the help of his loyal partner Sue, the old wooden deadwood was removed and replaced, although the grid had to be dug out to enable new bolts to be driven in. We were able to refit the whole rudder assembly, with a new rudder stock and bearing, welded to a new robust keel band. By mid December, to our great satisfaction, the job was complete and *Fairwater* could come off the grid on to her much more comfortable Winter mooring on the beach.

This, however, proved to be not the end of things but just the beginning. We asked Paul if he would come back in early January to have a look at two soft patches of decking and replace the old wheelhouse roof. In his usual thorough way, Paul revealed that not just the decking but a couple of deck beams had begun to rot through leakage of rainwater through the patches of soft decking. Instead of patching the damaged area, we joyfully decided to rebuild the whole maindeck over a new set of deck beams.

Paul and Sue worked for a couple of weeks in January to remove all the old decking, stanchions and the front frame of the wheelhouse and then we left everything to dry out under a tarpaulin for a couple of weeks, while I organized the materials for a rebuild. The old deck beams were laminated oak, which I had struggled to make myself out of the cheapest possible materials a few years before. As I pondered the best possible replacement for them, an advertisement appeared in the Western Morning News for baulks of pitchpine, which could be sawn to size. These turned out to be over 100 year old beams from a weaving factory in the Midlands, so as on inspection they proved to be absolutely sound, I ordered seven pieces of 11" x 4" x 14' long to be sawn and delivered, from which I reckoned I could saw out 14 curved beams of 4" x 4" beautiful honey coloured, indestructible pitchpine which could be varnished and not only provide the strength required, but which would be beautiful to look at and a structure which I was sure would have won the approval of Percy Mitchell, *Fairwater's* original builder.

Lifting these beams over the garden wall (just me and the lorry driver) then sliding them down the 60 odd steps to the quay, then setting them up in the workshop to be cut to shape with an electric saw which was designed to cut straight lines, rather than curved, and then planing, glass papering and decorating with mouldings gave me weeks of agony with a damaged back. But it was so worthwhile. Just to smell the beautiful pine resin of the timber, to feel its strength and durability and eventually to see it fitted and varnished, with the new deck above it gave rewards of satisfaction over and above the heavy work involved.

Paul meticulously laid two layers of marine plywood over these beams, which were varnished underneath, giving the whole cabin a beautiful warm deckhead and, in keeping with *Fairwater's* vintage, the deck outside was beautifully canvassed in traditional style with Egyptian cotton canvas, sealed and painted to make the ultimately waterproof deck.

With her new deck in such superb condition, of course we could not resist improving the hull underneath it. Old oak knees were replaced with galvanised iron brackets, the planking was reinforced where the legs bolted on, new cockpit floorboard bearers, new iroko cockpit seats and wash strakes, new laminated beams and decking for the wheelhouse roof, improved cabin furniture, new wiring for the eighteen lights on board, plus numerous supplies to electrical equipment, new hatches for the wheelhouse and fo'c'sle and, as a final touch, I made a new cabin table in varnished iroko.

It was July before all this work was completed and just to add full measure to our workload, from May onwards our house was invaded by a team of builders, who turned an old garage into a 'granny-flat' for my mother and re-roofed the house and the sunroom, with decisions and purchases to be made almost every day, on top of all the work on the boat.

How could all this effort, expense and stress be justified? Why, of course, just one more Summer in the Isles of Scilly, to arrive in our own boat, to meet our old friends and to cruise around as we chose, walking our beloved dogs on whatever island and in whatever weather conditions the good Lord sent us in 1982.

Chapter Twelve

1982 to 1985

All the frantic workload already described was helped throughout June and July by fine, settled, sunny weather. When we finally were ready to come off the beach, on the morning of Wednesday August 4th, the weather reverted to its normal August monsoon, just as I was walking the dogs after breakfast. Clouded skies began to produce spots of rain and the wind began to turn into a bad tempered southwesterly which boded ill for any trip down channel as planned, with young Philip Newton and the two dogs as crew. We punched into the head seas off Penlee and Rame and continued to pitch and roll for the next three hours down channel in the wind and the rain before we reached the shelter of Fowey harbour. Philip had disappeared to the cabin, prostrated with seasickness. The dogs looked miserably at me in the wheelhouse, clearly puzzled as to why their normally loving and sensible master was subjecting them to such endless discomfort.

All the crew recovered instantly once we had anchored and run ashore in the dinghy for a walk. Next morning in still cloudy but now better conditions with offshore winds of northwest force 3, we pressed on to St Mawes, anchoring off the Lugger Inn at Portloe for lunch on the way. Saturday and Sunday were spent in the Helford and St Mawes area, awaiting the arrival of my nephew Andrew Davy, who was to join us for the run to the Isles of Scilly. Then on Monday we had a routine run against the usual headwinds to St Mary's, taking just under nine hours of anxiety and discomfort to reach our anchorage in the harbour.

We spent the following week cruising around the Islands in poor weather, trying to find a reasonably quiet anchorage each night. Friday was Peggy's arrival day by air from Plymouth and we anchored in Porthcressa for Thursday night to shelter from a westerly force 4 to 6, which was then going to complicate things by going southwest and strengthening to force 8. We left Porthcressa at 06:45 before conditions got too bad and anchored in St Mary's harbour which is reasonably sheltered from the southwest. In spite of the poor weather, after Peggy arrived at the airport we all enjoyed a lunch at the Atlantic Inn and we left for St Agnes to spend the night in the Cove, which we reckoned would be sheltered as the wind turned more to the west overnight.

The next three days continued the pattern of wet, unsettled weather, with westerly winds up to and sometimes in excess of gale force. We spent one night with the forecast for southwesterlies of 7, 8 and 9 at Watermill Cove, which is our favourite retreat in such conditions and actually enjoyed a visit from our Island friends the Williams' and their French visitors during the day and enjoyed a steady, if noisy, night of continued gales until the morning of Wednesday August 18th.

This was the day when Philip Newton had to return to the Mainland, so we had to leave the shelter of Watermill to get him and his luggage within easy reach of *Scillonian III* in the harbour. We did the trip around the 'outside', the east and south coasts of St Mary's to Porthcressa in leisurely fashion, catching three dozen mackerel on the way, which provided a welcome feast for ourselves and our friends. Having waved farewell to Philip at 16:30 we headed for St Agnes for the night, but found conditions there so rolly that we ended up going all the way back to Watermill. There we enjoyed a clear quiet night.

On Thursday we had to return to St Mary's harbour, which was exposed to a west to northwest force 4 to 5, as we needed diesel fuel and a new gas cylinder for the galley. We also had the pleasure of an evening meal with our friends the Williams' but after the warmth and comfort and good food with them, we had to face the difficulties and dangers of taking a heavily laden dinghy off the beach at low tide into the darkness, the rain and the onshore breakers of a westerly gale.

Friday brought continued onshore winds into the harbour but the tide was right for a shrimping expedition to St Martin's Flats, where we struggled to make a moderate catch in the cold and windy conditions. Then, yet again, we had to retreat to Watermill Cove to find some shelter for the night. We had to leave there for the rough conditions of the harbour next day, because now it was Andrew's turn to be put on the *Scillonian III* for the journey back to the Mainland.

We ourselves returned on Wednesday August 25th for the run back to Helford with Paul and Nadia Williams as crew. By Saturday 28th we were back on our mooring in the Tamar having covered 357 miles in almost permanent bad weather.

Our Summer cruise to Scilly for 1983 was routine. We had worked so hard on the aftermath of the granny-flat extension to the house all Summer that Peggy and I decided we would not take any young friends or relatives as crew and we left the Tamar on Wednesday 27th July, returning on Saturday August 13th.

The 1984 cruise was very similar; from Thursday 26th July to Saturday August 18th. This proved to be a better than average visit from the weather point of view and we frequently enjoyed the company of our niece Jacki who was waitressing at the Atlantic Hotel for the Summer season. My wife and I needed a quiet holiday because apart from commitments at work, we had worked hard on improving the garden at home and Peggy was constantly caring for her 95 year old father who was in such ill health that he had to come to live permanently with us.

1985 proved to be the worst year yet from the point of view of the weather especially on Saturday 3rd August with the threat of a southwesterly force 8 and Sunday the 4th with southwesterlies becoming force 9 or 10 later and Monday the 5th, when the wind was to go around to the northwest and stay at force 10. In the small hours of this day we experienced the nearest thing to shipwreck that we ever had to face.

We were now quite experienced in sitting out bad weather in the shelter of Watermill Cove. The Cove has no facilities; no lights, no phone box and even its sandy beach turns to granite boulders clogged with rotting seaweed at high water level. What it does provide is a narrow indentation in the coastline, backed with a valley of Cornish elms, completely sheltered from the west. Gales still blow down this valley, with gusts that could hit *Fairwater* with explosive force, but it was immune from the Atlantic swell, which when driven by a normal westerly gale, would cause mayhem in St Mary's harbour.

We spent a couple of days resigned to letting the bad weather blow itself out. We landed for dogwalks and we watched quite a lot of television on our new set, without realising the drain this was causing to our main batteries. The very deep depression causing the winds of storm force 10 and severe storm force 11 mentioned by the shipping forecast did not worry us unduly but we were quite unprepared for the sudden change in direction which occurred after a lull about 01:00 or 02:00 which sent a northwest wind into the northeast, where it blew directly into the cove.

In the limited anchorage space, we found that a French yacht that had anchored on a long rope quite safely beside us, was now directly astern with her anchor warp now as taught as a violin string immediately under our keel, rudder and propeller. Steep seas made *Fairwater* pitch wildly in the darkness, threatening to take us and our French neighbour onto the jagged rocks astern. To raise our anchor and move out to sea in these conditions would be frightening enough but when I tried to start the Sabb engine which powered the anchor winch, there was no response: watching T.V had flattened the battery completely. The main Volvo diesel started immediately as normal but there was the probability that any use of it would tangle our propeller with the Frenchman's anchor rope and we would both be driven astern onto the rocks.

Fairwater was now burying her bow in the foaming breakers every few seconds and moving about the boat could only be achieved by hanging on tightly to avoid being thrown to the deck. The dogs looked pathetically at us in the dim lights from the cabin floor, their worried eyes asking us whatever we thought we were doing now, but loyal crew as they were, they kept still and did not panic.

My only option was to use the main diesel to keep the boat moving slowly ahead to take the strain off the anchor chain and wrestle with the steering wheel to make sure that we did not override our anchor chain or come broadside to the breaking seas. This process continued from 3 o'clock until 5 o'clock in the morning when the first signs of daylight appeared. While I was at the wheel Peggy had contacted the Coastguards ashore to warn them of a possible shipwreck situation and ask for assistance in raising our two anchors to enable us to clear the anchorage. All the Coastguard could do was to advise us to drop a third anchor if we had one. This we did have, stored under one of the fo'c'sle bunks, but it was a really heavy, old fashioned 'fisherman' pattern anchor, with heavy chain attached to it and the problem of dropping it was that Peggy would have to drag it back the length of the cabin and wheelhouse and then along the pitching deck, before dropping it off the bow when I drove the boat ahead into the seas. I could not leave the steering wheel and engine controls to assist. In normal conditions Peggy would not have been able to lift the anchor, let alone assemble it for use and throw it out from the bow. When in imminent danger of shipwreck however, the adrenalin flows and reserves of strength and energy appear from nowhere. Peggy dragged the anchor, with its chain and warp the length of the heaving maindeck and I drove the boat ahead before signalling when to drop it. We were now safe from driving ashore, but were immovably held by three anchors to ride out the storm.

Peggy's radio call to the Coastguard had been heard by our friend Roger Williams who had been called out on duty as an Auxiliary Coastguard. He said over the radio that he would come to assist us personally as soon as he came off duty at 6 o'clock. He also tried to arrange for help from a local salvage boat, but conditions in the harbour were so horrific that the crew of the boat could not get out to the mooring to bring us any assistance.

Roger himself arrived on board *Fairwater* after being given a lift out from the beach by a French inflatable dinghy, which we suspect had 'abandoned ship' at the height of the storm. Thanks to Roger's muscle power and determination, we retrieved all three anchors, while I helped as much as I could by powering the boat ahead to ease the strain. By 07:30 we were able to leave the anchorage and go around the 'outside' of St Mary's to find shelter in Porthcressa. At this stage the Volvo engine had been performing faultlessly for four hours at low revs, in conditions so rough that our propeller frequentl came out of the water, putting sudden strain on the stern gland and shaft. Al the hard work on the engine installation had proved to be worthwhile.

The last stage of the journey to Porthcressa, around Peninnis Head wa quite difficult and frightening, but once anchored close in to the beach, w were able to change the batteries over to start the Sabb diesel and then kee the engine running to charge them up. We spent the rest of the day recovering although the wind remained northerly, about force 7. This was the only tim we had ever felt it necessary to ask the Coastguard for assistance, althoug in the end, we had been able to solve our own problem, albeit with Roge Williams' stalwart assistance.

Early the next morning we left Porthcressa for the Mainland, bein prepared to have a rough ride up channel with the leftover swell of the gal pushing us along.

By 20:30 we were anchored off Durgan beach in the Helford river, havin made good 71.7 miles in nine and a quarter hours in spite of unfavourabl tide conditions.

The ship's log for the next day, Wednesday 7th August simply read "Quiet day off Durgan beach." On our return to the Tamar on Friday we ha covered 486 miles since the Spring bank holiday.

Of our eleven days in Scilly, we had only two days of winds forecast a less than force 6 and for three days we had endured winds of force 10 an 11. This poor weather, plus the stress of our near shipwreck began a bout o prolonged bronchitis and asthma, which led to my early retirement fron teaching by the end of the year. By coincidence Peggy was given voluntar redundancy from the Sun Alliance at the same time. In spite of my healt problem, we could now look forward to making a prolonged visit to th Isles of Scilly in June and July and return to base in the Tamar before th arrival of the August monsoon which had given us so much trouble in th past. With my asthma responding to treatment and a less stressful lifestyl we could now look forward to our best ever opportunity to spend time in ou beloved Islands. How I looked forward to just one more Summer there, bu with my poor state of health and an increasingly ageing *Fairwater*, I dare not push my hopes past the Summer of 1986.

Chapter Thirteen

1986

As if life already had not enough problems, the first fruits of enjoyable etirement were not helped when I badly injured my left knee when working on the T.V. aerial in the roof at home. Pegs helped me descend the loft ladder and the stairs to road level and drove me to the nearest casualty department, which at that time was in the Naval hospital at Devonport.

With my left leg rigid with agony, I managed with the help of two walking ticks to hop my way into the hospital, where a young Naval doctor completely mis-diagnosed my problem as a pulled hamstring. My G.P. doctor riend, Emrys Owen, later gave a more correct diagnosis, recognising torn igaments and tendons in the knee as the source of the problem.

After three weeks of agony on crutches and a week sleeping in a chair downstairs before I could enjoy the luxury of a night in a bed, I was able to imp along with the help of a walking stick when we went for a motoring holiday in France with my two brothers-in-law, Herbert and John.

Thanks to the help of a couple of ex-pupils, Shaun Stevens and John Woodley, work progressed on the quay and the dinghy platform and crane. We did the routine fitting out on *Fairwater* and in view of the workload and my injury, we were fortunate to be able to take her on the way to Scilly for et one more Summer on Monday, 9th June.

Peggy and the dogs remained at home, officially waiting for the repaired Nautech autopilot to arrive. Probably all three welcomed the chance for me o take *Fairwater* towards Scilly, with John Woodley as crew, with all the discomforts and worries of the trip, so that they could come across on *Scillonian III* later on. This proved to be a pretty long drawn out process.

Typically we set out at 17:00, to face the arrival of an Atlantic depression, with southwesterly gales, but as we had now put all our gear on board and were fit for sea, we were determined not to take the easy way out and return o the comforts of the house for the night but chose instead to leave the mooring and run up river to anchor off Cargreen. There we were able to pick up a mooring off the Spaniard's Inn and after a run ashore, settled into the outine of life on board, while we slept away a night of very heavy rain, heltered from the wind.

Tuesday was a bright, showery day, with squally winds gusting up to force 8 which one might expect after the clearance of a depression. We left Cargreen after breakfast and motored down to the mooring at Saltash Passage, where we were able to collect the long awaited autopilot, before going down to anchor in Barn Pool for lunch.

By a fortunate coincidence our old friends Frank and Gwen Smale walked to Barn Pool from their cottage at Empacombe and were soon brought out on board by John Woodley in the dinghy. This proved to be a fortunate coincidence in more ways than one, because John wanted to become an apprentice boatbuilder on leaving school and Frank and Gwen were good friends with the management of Mashford's boatyard at Cremyll. They were both taken by John's boating skills and his obvious love of wooden boats. Later on their good impression, plus my reference as one of John's teachers enabled him to be apprenticed at Mashford's, to everyone's satisfaction.

By Thursday we had pressed on as far as Fowey and on Friday headed for Falmouth. This was a Friday the 13th, a date of ill omen for seafarers and I felt depressed because amongst other things my father had died on a Friday 13th. But this was a beautiful sunny day with light variable winds and I looked up at the blue skies in a positive effort to cheer up. As I did so as we were heading for Dodman Point, a line of beautiful gannets passed us, heading out towards the sea and the sun in a perfect straight line formation. As I counted them, to my delight, there were exactly thirteen. What a cheering omen!

We spent a week in the Falmouth area, Peggy bringing the dogs down to join the crew for the trip to Scilly.

The next Friday brought a freak thunderstorm while we were at anchor off St Mawes. We watched the local Fire Brigade pump the floodwater out of the Jolly Sailor restaurant. Further thunderstorms drifted around in the evening and overnight bringing alternating patches of calm and squalls gusting to gale force.

Next morning we went up river in the rain, mainly to keep the engines and the crew occupied and anchored off Tolcarne Creek for lunch. As the afternoon went on it rained more and more heavily, but the dogs had to be walked and they were so drenched that when we returned, Ike slipped off the wet afterdeck into the swiftly ebbing river, to give a fine display of frantic dogpaddling to keep near us until he could be rescued from the dinghy. When we returned to St Mawes in the evening, the air was still full of rain and mist. Next morning the radio reported this day as the wettest June day ever recorded locally. Penzance recorded 52mm, over two inches of rain. Cornwall was suggested as having generally received about 200 tons of rain per acre

Ike, who was listening to the forecast nodded his head, agreeing that it had been his wettest day ever as well.

It was the middle of the next week before we had a shipping forecast reasonable enough to leave Helford for the Isles of Scilly. Even then we had a very rock and rolly time rounding the Lizard, which left the dogs legless with their form of seasickness, which they had to endure for many hours more when crossing from Land's End to Scilly.

A few dogwalks ashore and some inter-island cruising soon restored them to their normal cheerful selves. Saturday, June 28th saw us back in St Mary's harbour for crew change-over day, with John Woodley going back to the Mainland, and Peggy arriving on *Scillonian III* . Skip spent the next day or two all dreamy eyed and grinning with delight to have his beloved 'Mum' back on board again.

On Sunday we saw *Virgin Atlantic Challenger II* come into harbour after breaking the transatlantic crossing record. We dressed ship overall in honour of the occasion and all on board joined in the noisy welcome with foghorn, cheers, barks and howls.

We were then able to spend the next five and a half weeks cruising around our beloved Isles of Scilly, to achieve our lifetime dream of a long holiday afloat there. On the move nearly every day, with a succession of friends from ashore or from other boats, we never had a day of boredom and not too many days of uncomfortable weather.

We returned to the Mainland bronzed, happy and with some feeling of achievement, finally picking up our home mooring off Saltash Passage on Tuesday 12th August after living afloat for just over two months, covering 643 miles in the process. Oh! for just such another Summer next year!

We were not to know that the year ahead would produce a much better than usual weather pattern, making our next cruise even better.

Chapter Fourteen

Summer Cruise 1987

Apart from the normal laying up routine in the Autumn, Winter work on *Fairwater* was not too demanding this year, enabling us to fit in different projects during the off season. Firstly, I was able to cast a new two and a quarter ton hexagonal concrete and iron sinker for our new mooring in the river, which had now become one of a 'trot' of moorings holding boats fore and aft in place of the old swinging moorings which used to take up so much more room. In the process of renewing the mooring chains, I managed to slip on the seaweed while pulling a length of old chain up the beach. The leverage effect of slipping while pulling such a heavy weight, plus the fact that I instinctively put my right arm out to break the fall resulted in a complex series of shoulder/tennis elbow/golfer's elbow/rib/spine and collar bone injuries which gave me months of acute discomfort and a permanent weakness in my right collar bone joint.

Secondly we were able to take advantage of the spare time provided by retirement to visit friends in the Algarve in February and motor across France to go to a wedding in Italy, near Milan, before returning via Switzerland and the Loire Valley.

Fairwater was not forgotten, however, and after a visit to the London Boat Show in January she received a new Plastimo 'Atlantic' cooker for the galley and a Decca MK IV navigator to help us find our way to Scilly next Summer.

This was now the Summer of 1987 and we set out with a crew of just Peggy and myself and the two dogs. As usual Skip and Ike knew only too well when the boring preparations were complete at last and we were presented with the problem of controlling two ecstatic Springers, with the combined bodyweight of a hundredweight of muscle down the steep path and steps leading to our quay. Once there they had to be persuaded not to take their first celebratory swim, before boarding the little dinghy, where discipline immediately revived, for the journey out to *Fairwater* on her mooring, where it was impossible to judge whether humans or dogs were most pleased to be afloat again.

Having set out on Saturday, 13th June, we pottered about the Falmouth area until Monday, 29th June before we had a shipping forecast with wind strength and visibility suitable for a crossing to Scilly which would not distress crew or dogs too much. We reached St Mary's harbour in nine and a quarter hours in moderate headwind conditions and overcast skies which made arrival a much more pleasant experience than travelling in expectation.

Our arrival brought sunshine and quiet conditions and it was probably the same sunshine that gave us a treat a couple of days later, off Wingletang Ledge, St Agnes, when we spotted what we thought was a turtle, sunning itself on the surface of the sea. We gently approached to find a beautiful sunfish alongside, willing to be photographed and obviously enjoying the sunshine as much as ourselves. Some weeks later the Western Morning News angling feature proudly recorded the fact that a 53 pound sunfish had been caught, killed and photographed with its proud killer off the Cornish Coast. We were sad to think that it might be our beautiful sunfish that had come to such a sad and pointless end.

Then, for a week, we enjoyed the company of Harry and Syl Hughes on *Havssula*, a Laurent Giles 13 tonner. In generally sunny weather we cruised around and met up with them in all the usual anchorages. Saturday, 11th July to Tuesday 14th were ideal shrimping tides and we visited three different areas, to provide ourselves and our friends with prawn cocktails and prawn salads, delicacies made sweeter by the effort involved in catching them, with a freshness of flavour quite unknown to the frozen supermarket version.

We then enjoyed some heavenly days in the sunshine, anchored in The Cove, St Agnes until we woke up on Sunday morning to hear the soft sound of rain drumming on the deck. After breakfast it was still raining, but dogs have to be walked regardless of weather. On the road to the lovely old lighthouse we contacted a local farmer and negotiated for a sackful of White Lion bulbs to take back to Plymouth with us to transform the flower beds on our terrace into a Scillonian carpet in the early Spring. He gladly put his wet weather gear on and then brought the bulbs down to the Bar beach on his tractor. Where else in the world would such a cheerful deal be completed on a wet Sunday morning? We raised anchor at 10:30 to seek the shelter of Porthcressa as showers and gusts of force 7 continued for the rest of the day. Whatever else happened, *Fairwater* had her sack of bulbs stowed away in place of a sackful of dogfood that Skip and Ike had consumed.

After a day trip to St Martin's on Tuesday, we joined *Havssula* to explore the archaeological site on Nornour in ideal sunny conditions, with just a gentle northerly breeze. We took several photos of this site, which was only found following a storm damage cliff fall in 1962. The complex walls of the houses are typical Iron Age construction and a great quantity of metal objects, mainly brooches and figurines were found, together with a considerable number of Roman coins AD70 to AD380. The finds included 30 finger rings,

6 bracelets and almost 300 decorative brooches. This unique site, so atmospheric and so unprotected fascinated me then and draws me back each year to speculate on its special significance.

After enjoying St Agnes' Cove for one last day, we left the Scillies for the Mainland on Friday, 24th July, gently travelling from the Helford to St Mawes and Fowey, to return to our mooring on the Tamar on the following Thursday. There we were able to install our long awaited Decca MK IV navigator and sort out a list of minor defects, before taking the two lads who had worked so hard on *Fairwater*, for a week's trip to Helford and back as a gesture of thanks for all their efforts. This virtually brought the 1987 season to an end. Peggy had now been treated to a good quality camera for her 60th birthday, and *Fairwater's* log books which were conscientiously written up each day during the Summer and then rewritten in the following Winter, now recorded our dozens of detailed colour photographs which are a joy to look back on.

Chapter Fifteen

Some detail of the work involved in fitting out *Fairwater* for her role as Summer home afloat might be of interest to anyone not having experienced the mixture of excitement and desperation brought about by this annual labour of love.

In 1988 it took seven weeks of dedicated work. Hours of painting of the hull, the bilges, the ballast blocks and the bottom. This proceeded when weather permitted on the exposed beach at the bottom of the garden.

Some verses might capture the atmosphere of the work involved:

Dream Voyage

Icy wind screams down the Tamar, due north from Kit Hill,
White horses flee down the river, from the blast's icy chill,
While there on the beach, where the mud meets the sand,
A fool stands half frozen, paint brush in his hand.

His eyes fill with tears, but not caused by sadness;
They water with cold, because of the madness
Of painting his boat, while the wind blows away
The paint from his brush in an untidy spray.

The fool, he is smiling, his eyes full of dreams,
While the coat of blue paint hides the boat's old cracked seams,
But his mind's far away and that's why he smiles
In the sunshine and heat of the 'Fortunate Isles'.

For several weeks later, as habit demands
The boat and its owner head for Scilly's gold sands:
And the rocks and the Isles and the sea blue and green,
The nearest thing to heaven his eyes ever have seen.

But the work must start early, there's so much to do,
To make the boat safe for himself and his crew,
As they head out of the Tamar and sail to the west
On the course down the Channel which he knows is best.

The dangers of bad weather and tides never end,
Past the Dodman and Lizard and down to Land's End.
The long trip past the Wolf and the dangers of fog
Until we reach Scilly, a hundred miles on the log.

But don't go too quickly, there's room for delay;
Don't sail on past Fowey; call in for a day.
Cut close to the Dodman and then if you wish
Sail slowly to Falmouth and catch a few fish.

And stay at St Mawes if the wind's in the east,
To soak up the sunshine for one day at least.
Then sail on to Helford, most beautiful sight
And anchor off Durgan for a starry calm night.

And then if a gale blows up from the west
The anchorage at Helford is really the best.
There safe from the wind see the river's green charms
And dry from the rain in the old Shipwright's Arms.

Then listen to forecasts at o five fifty five
If safely to Scilly you wish to arrive.
Don't mess with the Lizard or his anger arouse
He'll hit you with waves as big as a house.

You'll find when he's asleep if you use the tide table;
Keep well out to sea; as far out as you're able.
Relax for the run across Mount's lovely Bay
Past the Wolf head for Scilly the rest of the day:

The world's greatest thrill, search wherever you might
As the long day goes on, the Isles come into sight.
For you've made it to Heaven and on your own boat
You're the happiest and proudest man that's afloat.

That night in the harbour, sky velvety black
Soft voices come from the Islands to welcome you back.
As you look at the sea and the bright stars above,
The Islands surround you and hold you with love.

So back to the fool with a brush in his hand,
Not dreaming at sea, he's stuck on the dry land.
He's made a step forward, one less job to be done
And when freezing in Winter he's worshipped the sun.

Apart from the routine painting and varnishing, improvements were made to the battery charging and gas supply systems. Masts, rigging, sails, anchor winch, anchor chains and the two dinghies had to be checked and refurbished. Finally stowage had to be found for the tins, bottles, bedding, vegetables, fruit and dog food. Then there remained the last minute searching for flags and charts, fishing lines and fenders; the topping up of diesel tanks, water tanks, petrol cans, the stowage of outboards: all had been done by the morning of Wednesday 18th May.

The grey skies and chilly northeasterly wind did not cool the enthusiasm of the dogs to go to sea yet again and we had the usual problem of restraining them on our steps down to the quay without being pulled over, or pulled apart in the process. An hour or two later all their enthusiasm had gone. As we pitched and rolled our way down channel towards Looe and Polperro they made it very obvious that they had tired of this seagoing business and with big, sad, enquiring eyes they asked us to head for the delights of the nearest land, rather than heroically struggle with the long stretches of unfriendly seas. Real seadogs do not weaken in this fashion, but Skip and Ike, as always, provided us with an excuse to head in for the shelter of Fowey, instead of pressing on for another three or four hours to reach Falmouth.

We found the anchorage at Fowey pleasantly deserted at this early stage of the season and when we picked up a visitor's mooring the harbour master's patrol boat came alongside and he found time for a friendly chat. After making a fuss of the dogs and collecting the dues, he gave us a large pen and ink portrait of his own Spaniel. It was so good to be back in dear old friendly Fowey, with its busy scene of commercial shipping mixed with pleasure boating watched over by 'Q's monument up on the Hall Walk. We soon took the dinghy in to the landing below the monument and we all rejoiced in the steep climb through the wild Spring flowers to the path that overlooks 'Q's beloved Troy Town.

On returning to the dinghy we crossed the harbour to the recently provided pontoon which gave easy access to the streets and shops of Fowey. The day's run of four hours had covered only twenty five miles, but we were richly rewarded with our walks, our evening meal on board and the knowledge that our boat, engines and equipment were all working properly.

The next day we moved on to St Mawes and from there went on to the Isles of Scilly on Friday, arriving at 17:30, finding it easy to anchor in our favourite spot as we were the only visiting yacht in the harbour. Next came the happy routine of walking the dogs around the Garrison Walls on St Mary's, reporting our arrival to Island friends, who knew already because of the information network between Islanders which is one of Scilly's charms, phoning home to report our safe arrival and finally, enjoying our evening meal on board in the sunshine. Being Friday, we saw the gig race finish at the Pier Head and then watched a vivid red sun set between the two hills of Samson, all making us feel so pleased that we had really arrived.

As blue skies and southwesterly winds continued for the next few days, more boats arrived from the Mainland and ashore, Scilly's genius for providing the unexpected appeared in the shape of the Cornwall Police Band whose forty or so musicians made the granite buildings reverberate with such loud music and drumming that Skip tried to drown the noise with his own frantic barking.

We spent several days in the harbour as the southerly winds rose to force six and seven, conditions which make the harbour a perfect shelter and we were able to tackle a problem that had developed on our trip down: a malfunctioning ship's toilet. We hoped to remove this essential bit of equipment and take it ashore for the Isles of Scilly Steamship Company's engineers to tackle. They sensibly declined this dubious honour, but offered the loan of a large wrench with which we could disconnect it from *Fairwater's* Hull. When we had successfully lifted it through the cabin and into the cockpit, Peggy decided to tackle it herself, with a screwdriver and considerable enthusiasm. Then, after the application of several buckets of seawater and much vigorous pumping, the blockage was removed and normal service was resumed, to our great relief.

As we discovered next day, the Island communication service had been humming with concern for our predicament and then with joy for our eventual success. Nearly everyone to whom we said "Good morning" returned the greeting and added "I'm pleased to hear you've got your toilet sorted out". Such is the loving concern of the Scillonians for seafarers in a state of distress.

We had planned to go to St Helen's Pool next day, but we postponed the trip because the weather was cold, cloudy and windy from the southwest and the forecast at midday confirmed the wisdom of our decision as gale warnings for force 8 southwesterlies were issued for Plymouth and Sole sea areas. This called for a repeat of our well tried strategy of leaving the harbour for the eastern coast of St Mary's and the shelter of Watermill Cove. We moved just before lunch time and anchored close to the Cove beach, with only one small French boat anchored well out for company. Our lunch was accompanied by a downpour of rain while strengthening winds screamed through the rigging, buffetting *Fairwater* in the gusts. This small sheltered patch of sea remained calm, however, so we were not subjected to the rock and roll which the Atlantic would by now have begun to send into St Mary's harbour.

In a break in the weather we walked the dogs along paths with luxuriant wild flowers, the green verges spangled with red, white, blue and yellow. Back on board the rain became heavier, but we were snug and dry in the cabin and a good hot evening meal provided good cheer for the crew. Then later in the evening the weather improved from absolutely miserable to mildly unpleasant, the heavy rain being replaced by gale driven drizzle. We had to take the dogs ashore for routine exercise, so we walked them up to the Coastguard Tower, where we phoned home to tell them what vile weather was on the way. Once back on board the wind eased to about force 5 and by four o'clock in the morning it had died away altogether. One benefit of the Isles of Scilly's exposed position is that the Atlantic gales, however severe, seem to pass very quickly.

The improving weather enabled us to wander between the Islands with various friends culminating in a Friday evening meal with our great friends Roger and Alba in their beautiful granite walled dining room. These luxurious surroundings had to be left behind while we launched our dinghy over the sand and into the surf to find our way through the darkness and the breaking seas, to our home afloat for the night.

By morning, the squalls and showers had merged into a continuous downpour of rain thickened with fog and driven by southwesterly winds of gale force. We put on our heaviest waterproof suits to go ashore, while the dogs' curls turned to shiny wet matting as they got thoroughly soaked. But even more sorry looking were the passengers from the early morning *Scillonian* who had left Penzance at six thirty. Two ambulance loads of them were so sick they had to be taken to hospital, while others, soaking, white faced and some in tears trudged through the rainswept streets of Hugh Town, many clad in their clothing only fit for a sunny day on the beach. We returned on board *Fairwater* to enjoy rich, thick crab sandwiches made with fresh crabs bought the day before from a fishing boat. Then typical of rapidly changing Scillonian weather, the afternoon became brilliantly sunny and we all dried off walking to the Bronze Age settlement site at Bant's Carn.

In improving weather, our next visit was to the island of Bryher, where the film 'Why The Whales Came' was being shot, starring Paul Schofield, David Suchet and Helen Mirren. The whole film was shot on location and we found the cottage of the 'Birdman' with its beehives and chicken coops and we walked through the open door to the single crude room inside with the model sailing boat and the carved birds on the workbench, which all played a part in the story. Down the hill, towards the Pool, we found the filmset harbour with its nets and old fashioned crab pots, with bearded actors and local children in Edwardian costume preparing for filming.

We have often played our video recording of this film, especially when visited by young friends who have been to Scilly with us and its atmosphere and musical background have always transported us to the Islands that we came to love so much.

Over the next few days we moved between various anchorages which had to be chosen for shelter from the westerly winds which, as forecast, were force 6 or 7, making exciting conditions for some friends from Plymouth who came out with us. At least we could enjoy the shelter of the wheelhouse and spare some sympathy for the passengers on the open tripper boats who were generously treated to wind and spray in spite of their skipper's zigzag courses, to try to keep either bows or stern onto the seas. We ended up in Porthcressa, lying to an anchor and kedge in rather rolly conditions, until the wind, as forecast, went from west to northwest in the late evening. On leaving my bunk at about three a.m. just after high tide to do a routine check on conditions I was delighted to see that the swell had disappeared and a nearly full moon, low in a clear starlit sky, covered the now calm waters of Porthcressa with reflected moonlight.

Days turned into weeks while we moved around the Islands, sometimes giving hospitality to our Island friends on board and sometimes enjoying hospitality ashore in return.

On one morning dogwalk ashore on St Mary's, when the island was shrouded in fog we heard the mellow tones of trumpets and brass instruments and looking through the fog from the top of Buzza Hill we could see the children from the local school, standing like toy soldiers on a toy castle tower, playing their happy music to the town from the top of the church tower. A uniquely Scillonian event, memorable and moving.

It was Wednesday 28th June when we eventually left Scilly for the Mainland, with a couple of bags of 'Dutch Master' and 'Golden Harvest' Spring bulbs from St Agnes on board. We then spent several days in the Helford River as the weather deteriorated, before we finally returned to our mooring in the Tamar on Thursday 7th July.

We had covered 450 miles and we enjoyed 31 fine and dry days out of our 37 days in the Scillies, mainly thanks to a continuous spell of 26 days of high pressure weather in June, with easterly winds which gave sheltered conditions in St Mary's harbour. We had enjoyed anchoring around the Islands on 48 occasions, with the electric anchor winch taking the backache out of the process and all our mechanical, electrical and navigational gear had performed faultlessly. We felt grateful to *Fairwater* for returning us from our seven weeks of safe and comfortable holiday, with never a dull moment.

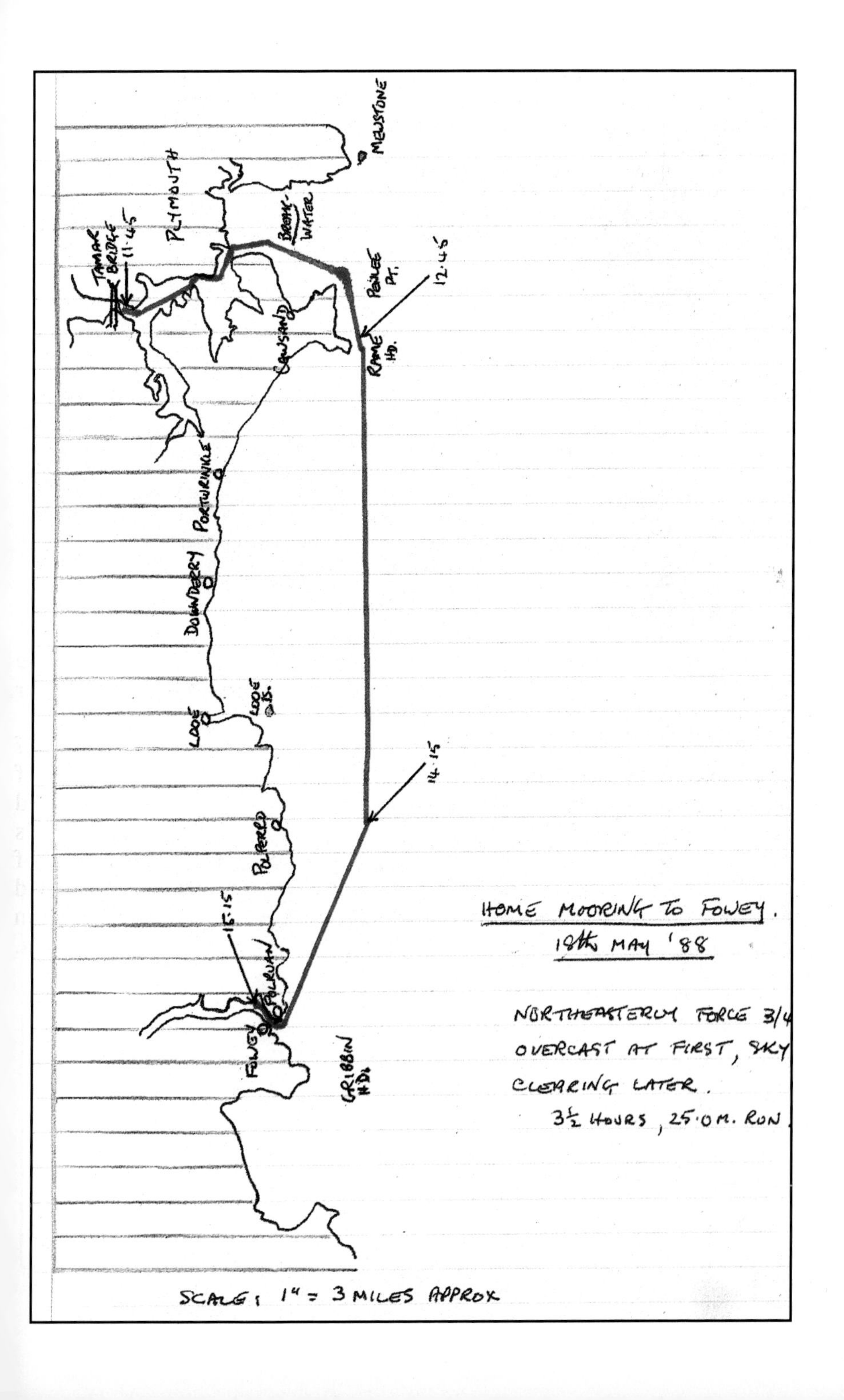
MEWSTONE
PLYMOUTH
BREAK-WATER
TAMAR BRIDGE
11.45
PENLEE PT.
12.45
CAWSAND
RAME HD.
PORTWRINKLE
DOWNDERRY
LOOE
LOOE IS.
14.15
POLPERRO
15.15
POLRUAN
FOWEY
GRIBBIN HD.
HOME MOORING TO FOWEY.
18th MAY '88
NORTHEASTERLY FORCE 3/4
OVERCAST AT FIRST, SKY
CLEARING LATER.
3½ HOURS, 25.0 M. RUN.
SCALE: 1" = 3 MILES APPROX

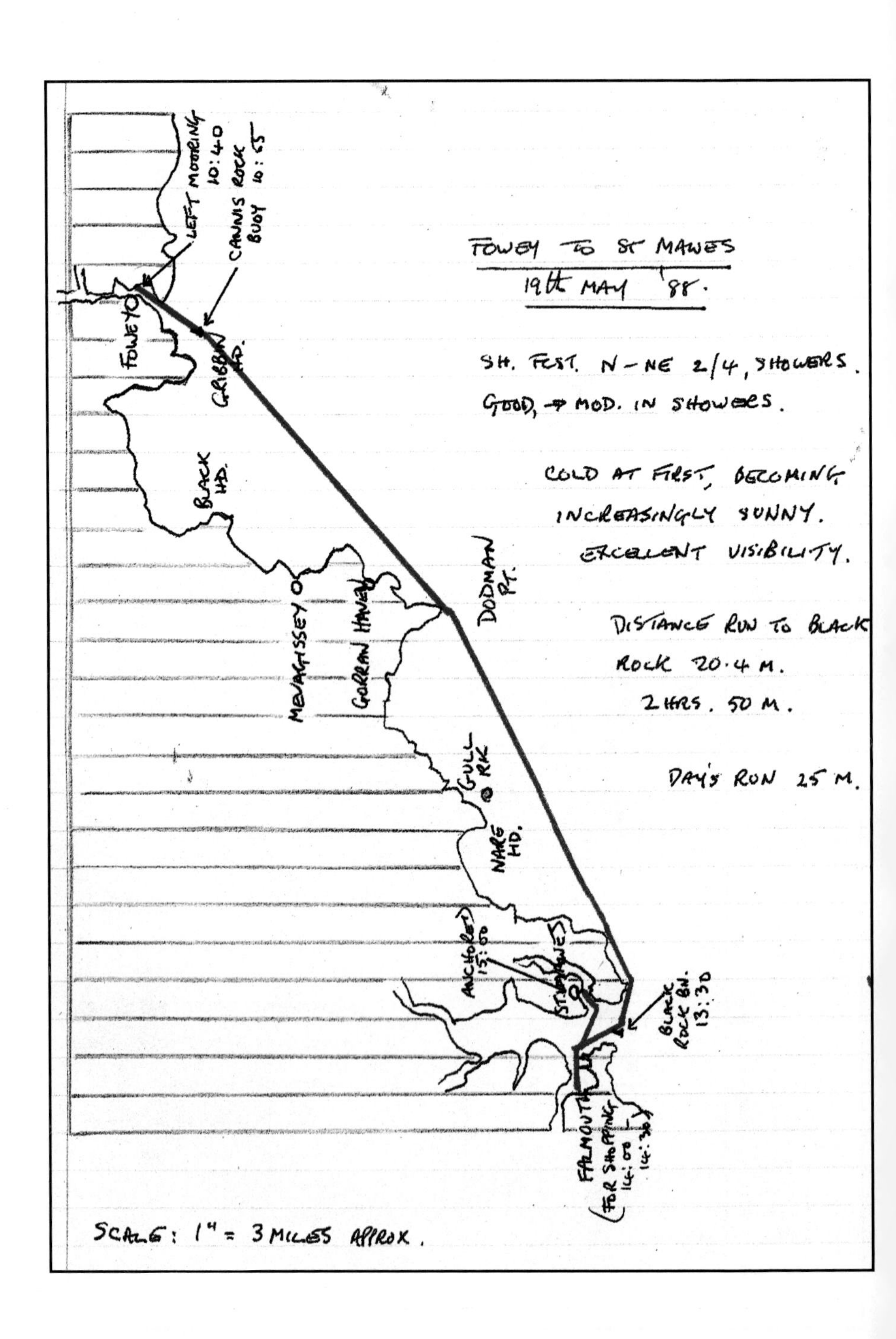
FOWEY TO ST MAWES
19th MAY '88.
SH. FCST. N–NE 2/4, SHOWERS.
GOOD, → MOD. IN SHOWERS.
COLD AT FIRST, BECOMING INCREASINGLY SUNNY.
EXCELLENT VISIBILITY.
DISTANCE RUN TO BLACK ROCK 20.4 M.
2 HRS. 50 M.
DAY'S RUN 25 M.
LEFT MOORING 10:40
CANNIS ROCK BUOY 10:55
FOWEY
GRIBBIN HD.
BLACK HD.
MEVAGISSEY
GORRAN HAVEN
DODMAN PT.
GULL RK
NARE HD.
ANCHORED 15:00
ST MAWES
BLACK ROCK BN. 13:30
FALMOUTH
(FOR SHOPPING 14:00 – 14:30)
SCALE: 1" = 3 MILES APPROX.

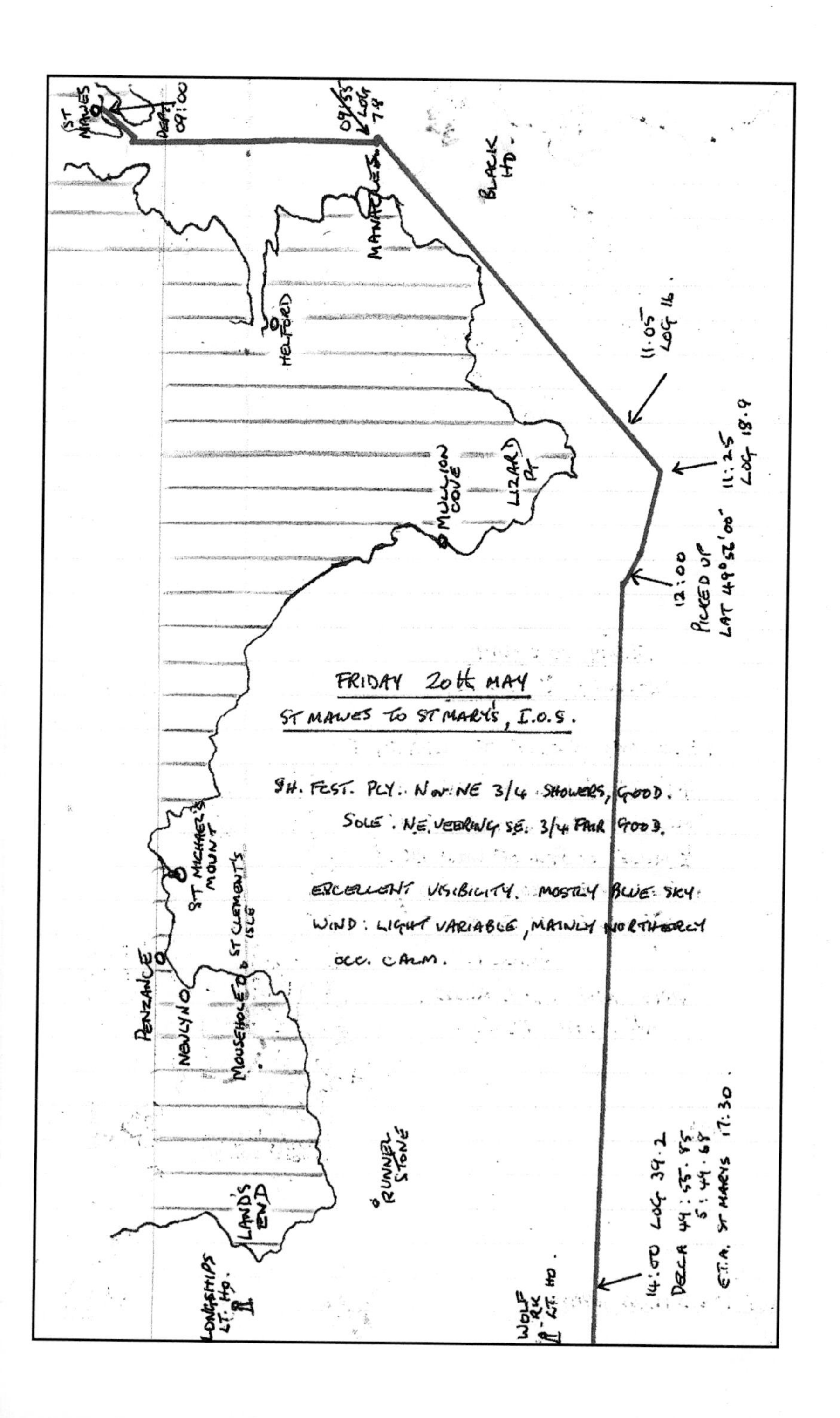

FRIDAY 20th MAY
ST MAWES TO ST MARY'S, I.O.S.
SH. FCST. PLY. N or NE 3/4 SHOWERS, GOOD.
SOLE. NE VEERING SE. 3/4 FAIR GOOD.
EXCELLENT VISIBILITY. MOSTLY BLUE SKY
WIND: LIGHT VARIABLE, MAINLY NORTHERLY
OCC. CALM.
ST MAWES
DEPT 09:00
09:55 LOG 7.8
BLACK HD.
MANACLES
HELFORD
11:05 LOG 16.
MULLION COVE
LIZARD PT
11:25 LOG 18.9
12:00
PICKED UP
LAT 49°52'00"
ST MICHAEL'S MOUNT
ST CLEMENT'S ISLE
PENZANCE
NEWLYN
MOUSEHOLE
RUNNEL STONE
LAND'S END
LONGSHIPS LT. HO.
WOLF RK LT. HO
14:00 LOG 39.2
DECCA 49:55.85
5:49.68
E.T.A. ST MARYS 17:30.

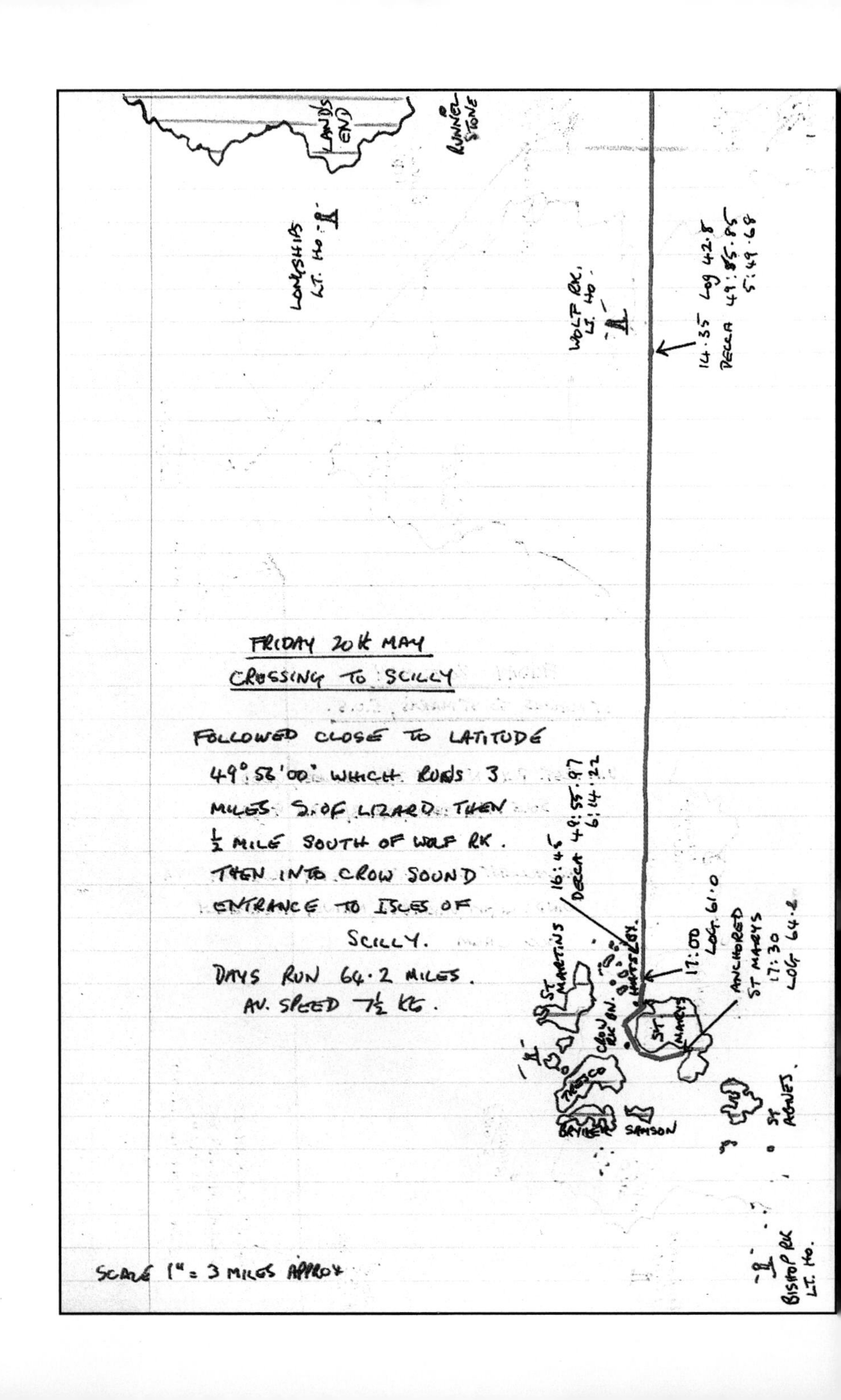
LANDS END
RUNNEL STONE
LONGSHIPS LT. HO.
WOLF RK. LT. HO.
14.35 LOG 42.8
DECCA 49:55.85
5:49.68
FRIDAY 20th MAY
CROSSING TO SCILLY
FOLLOWED CLOSE TO LATITUDE
49° 56' 00" WHICH RUNS 3
MILES S. OF LIZARD. THEN
½ MILE SOUTH OF WOLF RK.
THEN INTO CROW SOUND
ENTRANCE TO ISLES OF
SCILLY.
DAYS RUN 64.2 MILES.
AV. SPEED 7½ KTS.
16:46
DECCA 49:55.97
6:14.22
17:00
LOG 61.0
ANCHORED
ST MARYS
17:30
LOG 64.2
ST MARTINS
CROW RK BN.
HATS BOY.
ST MARYS
TRESCO
BRYHER
SAMSON
ST AGNES
BISHOP RK LT. HO.
SCALE 1" = 3 MILES APPROX

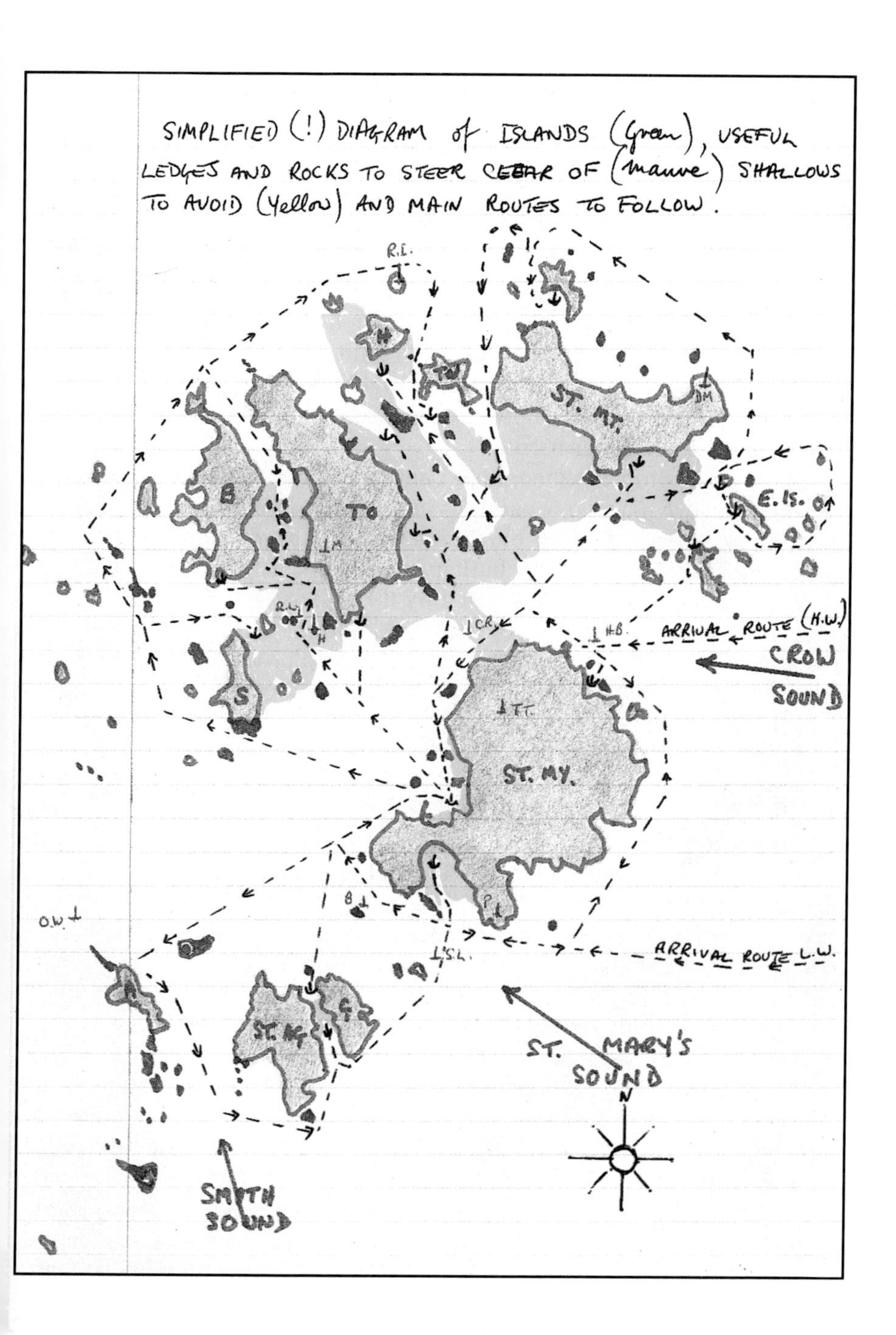

SIMPLIFIED (!) DIAGRAM of ISLANDS (Green), USEFUL LEDGES AND ROCKS TO STEER CLEAR OF (mauve) SHALLOWS TO AVOID (Yellow) AND MAIN ROUTES TO FOLLOW.
R.I.
H
TW
ST. MT.
DM
B
TO
M
E. IS.
R.W.
H
CR
HB
ARRIVAL ROUTE (H.W.)
CROW SOUND
T.T.
S
ST. MY.
B
F
P
O.W.
S.L.
ARRIVAL ROUTE L.W.
ST. AG
G
ST. MARY'S SOUND
N
SMITH SOUND

Chapter Sixteen

1989 and 1990

We put in four Winter months of continuous work this year, because the project was to jack *Fairwater* up high enough to burn off all the old bottom paint so that all the seams and planking could be checked. The hull would then have the opportunity to dry out thoroughly, any necessary repairs could be carried out and then the bottom could be repainted and antifouled to a higher standard than ever before.

This sounds simple in theory but I have the knack of making simple jobs complicated so *Fairwater's* painting turned into an excuse to improve the facilities we already had on our beach. We had a grid with five concrete crossmembers which we had built twelve years before. They were now suffering some wear and tear caused by the effects of the tides, winds and waves that covered them twice every day. Although *Fairwater* always floated in easily on the high Spring tides, the jacking up process was always slow and difficult, relying on constant wedging of the boat's legs to keep her upright. This process was not only tedious but it became increasingly dangerous with every inch of height we gained. *Fairwater's* registered tonnage was thirteen and although she did not actually weigh that much, any slip up in the jacking process could have fatal results for anyone working underneath her.

A wall was built against the existing rock face, with a wooden framework anchored to it which would make it impossible for the boat to fall over. Forty tons of concrete blocks and poured concrete went into the wall, all of which had to be manhandled sixty feet down from road level and the wooden framework had to be thirteen feet high by twenty four feet wide, with the heavy beams securely bolted to the uprights.

By the end of February, thanks to a reasonably dry and mild Winter, *Fairwater* was floated in to the new structure and jacked up a couple of feet (this took a day and a half to do) so that work could proceed. Our shipwright friend, Paul Dunbar, assisted with all the construction work and then burned off all the old antifouling paint. Paul's training as a shipwright had been in the hard school of coping with wooden fishing boats in Cornwall, with the minimum of boatyard facilities. This probably explained why he survived while burning off this poisonous paint as he lay underneath with his sturdy bearded frame becoming enveloped in clouds of dirt and smoke. A great believer in Cornish independence, an expert in the Cornish language, an enthusiast for trying to set up, single handed, a Cornish vineyard, a great raconteur of funny stories and a lover of Cornish and Breton folk music, *Fairwater* was lucky to have his talents and indomitable spirit at her disposal.

The heavy iron rudder was removed and repaired to improve its old worn bearings. I concentrated on woodwork improvements in the cabin and Phil and Geoff, our electronics experts updated our radio, navigation and generating systems.

Finally repainted, *Fairwater* left the grid on April 7th and then sat on the beach for the normal fitting out programme before being put on the mooring, ready for sea on May 16th. True to form we left the Tamar for the cruise to Scilly next morning, shrouded in fog, making a passage to St Mawes by mid afternoon feeling grateful for our Decca navigation system that told us exactly where we were every few seconds when we could not see where we were with the bad visibility.

We went early to bed after giving the dogs a good walk ashore, intending to make use of the favourable shipping forecast (force 3 to 4 easterlies) which would help us on our way. We did in fact make a record passage to St Mary's in eight hours, anchoring in our usual spot and pleased to see that we were the only visiting yacht there. When we took the dogs ashore, we found that the local communications system was as good as ever. Our friends the Pickups said

"Saw you come in from the car". Their son said

"Saw you come in from the workshop"; when we saw Alba at Tregarthen's Hotel where she was receptionist she said

"Roger saw you come in from the school". Jim Williams, the ex harbourmaster said next day

"Saw you come in from the quay" and on Saturday Eric Woodcock stopped his bus in Hugh Street, leaned out of the window and said

"Saw you come in and waved my club to you from the golf course". No wonder we soon felt at home having dropped our anchor

"In the same hole you dug last year" as our boatbuilder friend Tom Chudleigh said. We talked to John Nicholls, the new Trinity House Pilot for the Islands, who has replaced our old friend Roy Guy, who, sadly died during the Winter: of course

"Saw you come in" he said.

Our ten year old great nephew Philip joined us for the Spring bank holiday week from May 26th to June 2nd. He arrived excited by his first unaccompanied flight, from St Just in the little Skybus aircraft, where he insisted on passing his packet of peppermints to all the other passengers and the pilot!

The evening of his return was bright and sunny, the 'Islander' aircraft arrived on time and to our surprise was piloted by Dick Songer, a friend of ours, who offered Philip the co-pilot's seat for the flight back. We were sad to see him go because he had been such a good crew and while we were waiting at the airport he said he would go to the shop to buy some sweets and returned, in his gentlemanly ten year old way with a bunch of flowers for Peggy. These flowers added colour to our cabin for some time and refreshed our memories of his happy and sunny stay with us.

His return to the Mainland left us feeling that life would now slow down but life in Scilly is never dull. The next day, Saturday 3rd June happened to be the day that H.R.H. Prince Charles came to St Mary's for the official link up ceremony for the Islands' electricity supply by cable from the Mainland Peggy, with our friend Alba went to the quay to see him land in the Dorrien Smith's launch *Melledgan* while I opted to get on with the routine chores on board. As usual most of the Islanders chose to do the same as me, believing in giving the Royals the same right of privacy as any other visitor. The handful of spectators greeted Charles in a typically laid back way, before the Royal Procession went to the old generating station, the cavalcade consisting of a Peugeot with a broken number plate followed by a locally owned Land Rover

We took Roger and Alba with us on Sunday morning to the peace and solitude of The Cove at St Agnes to recover from such heady excitement and after lunching on board and dogwalking on the island in the afternoon, we returned to *Fairwater* for tea, which was delayed when we saw an empty G.R.P. dinghy drifting past us towards the open sea. We retrieved it and returned it to the beach. We shortly afterwards found it to be the tender to a large motorsailer from Cork anchored nearby. We then had an entertaining visit from the crew of four Irishmen who came to thank us and explain in a most hilarious fashion that their dinghy had been swept seawards as they had been "unavoidably detained" all the afternoon in the Turk's Head. We watched them motor away in the late afternoon sunshine heading for the Bishop lighthouse and the long voyage back to Ireland. We returned to S Mary's to anchor in Porthcressa Bay for the night.

The following weeks passed with the unique Scillonian mix of experience crayfish salad and Blanc de Blancs anchored in Rushy Bay; watching the gig crews race from Nut Rock in a downpour of rain and a force 8 gale followed by a rapid change when the cloud broke and the rain ceased, with the setting sun burning red through the torn clouds over Samson; collecting shells from the best beaches which later made a shell picture of a bunch of flowers still treasured today; dressing *Fairwater* all over in her signal flag to celebrate the launch of Tom Chudleigh's latest gig *Islander* to the accompaniment of noisy jollifications from all the other boats nearby, with

Fairwater in the lovely tranquil upper reaches of the river Tamar,

having passed one of the bends just down river from Morwellham.

Winter work proceeds, with Fairwater jacked up on the grid.

Paul Dunbar and I did necessary repair work to the deck.

We found that the 'Zodiac' inflatable dinghy would stow on deck if partially deflated.

Down below the varnishwork gleams in Fairwater's cosy cabin.

Seagulls, in the harbour

and in Porthcressa.

Colourful hedges on Tresco,

in comparison with the stark black and white of the lighthouse on Peninnis.

Ruins on the uninhabited island of Tean.

Hell Bay, on the north coast of Bryher.

Rosemary Codd in her canoe Salamander. Rose's talents with the word processor and with critical advice turned my scribble into a book.

The gorse blazes on Bryher where, incidentally, Rose spent her childhood.

Stalwart friends from the Tamar visit me when I settle in Scilly: Ron Gray, with his wife Vi.

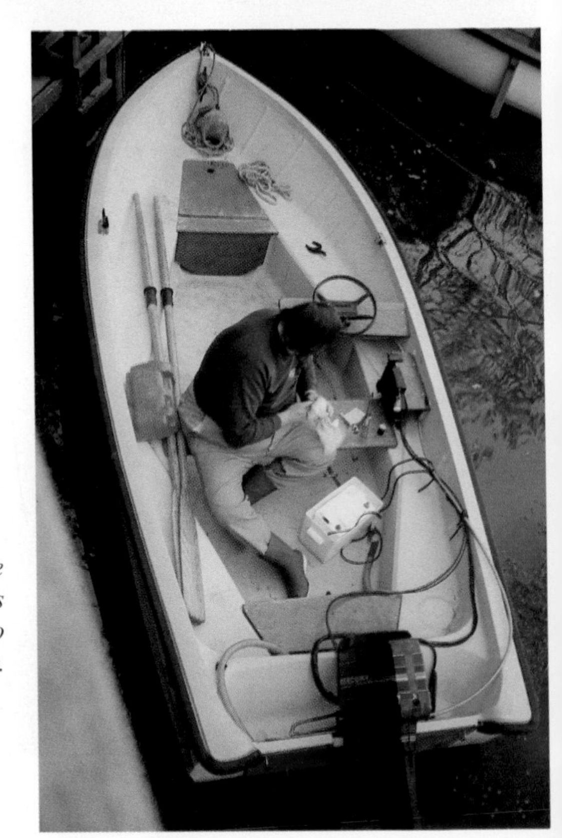

Phil Robins still working on the 'With' runabout which takes us all around the Islands so efficiently.

Fairwater arriving at her mooring as seen from the house: Coombe Creek railway viaduct opposite.

After Fairwater was sold, this outboard runabout was to provide transport around the Islands.

The holiday flat 'Lower Ganilly' (ground floor) which replaced Fairwater as our base in Scilly.

The dining table laid for a celebratory meal.

Our good friend Tom Chudleigh beside the fishing boat he built for himself, Mary M.

We saw her lifted from his boatyard and transported to the beach by two local trucks.

Fairwater at Clovelly Bay Marina, Plymouth, where she was offered for sale.

Fairwater with schoolchildren during an 'activities week' outing.

Great nephew Philip, one of Fairwater's

most regular crew members.

Fairwater's cabin, with the starboard side converted into a cargo hold with items for the flat.

Mobird, the inflatable dinghy with its own retractable wheels, which was so useful in Scilly.

Bay Tree Cottage at Old Town St. Mary's, my much loved final home.

Old Town church, across the bay where Peggy's ashes were finally placed.

Old Town harbour, with Mobird on a running line mooring.

Our last view of Fairwater after we sold her, on a mud berth at Weir Quay on the Tamar.

blasts on the foghorn and subsequent barks and howls from the dogs; the arrival of our friends the Hughes on *Havssula* with trips around the Islands with them, with hospitality given and returned on both boats and memorable meals ashore for both crews, enjoying the delicious fish meals at the 'Galley' restaurant.

In this way, the holiday which began in mid May now extended towards the end of June. In one patch of bad weather, after a night at anchor off Old Grimsby, we came across a very large inflatable dinghy, with nobody on board, blowing through St Mary's Roads and heading for the rocks of the Eastern Islands. We took it in tow, reported our find by radio to St Mary's Harbourmaster and towed it in to find it was adrift from a cruise liner, where it was used to ferry passengers ashore from *Polaris* on special expeditions organized from Fifth Avenue, New York. We obviously had a valuable salvage claim if we chose to pursue it but happily accepted a donation to the local R.N.L.I. instead, giving us the pleasure of putting a cheque for £100 into the funds.

When July arrived, we made use of the shrimping season for a day or two and then we opted to return to the Mainland in spite of a forecast of easterly headwind conditions. We paid for this decision by enduring a long and uncomfortable trip back, taking over eleven hours compared with the eight hours it took to come down. When rounding the Lizard, always a bad passage in easterly conditions, Peggy had to sit on the cockpit floor with an arm around each of our dogs who were by now legless with seasickness, to save them being thrown about with the vicious rocking and rolling of the boat. Five minutes ashore and the dogs recovered, but the crew were very tired and stressed by the long trip.

Yet again we enjoyed leisurely visits to Helford, St Mawes and Fowey on our way back to the Tamar, where we came into our own beach moorings on Thursday 13th July. We had been on board for eight weeks and covered 460 miles. Yet again the winter's work had been repaid with a long, trouble free holiday in the Islands we had come to love so much.

Peggy and I had now been retired for five years and retirement had given us time to improve *Fairwater* in her role as a safe and comfortable home afloat. The routine had become established that we would leave Tamar for Scilly in the middle of May each year, the exact day being chosen well in advance to give us the maximum help from the down channel tides after early morning starts. This routine worked again very well in 1990 and we enjoyed the same sort of boating and socialising as before, to the delight of the dogs and the young crews who joined us from time to time.

The only major work on *Fairwater* for the 1990 season was to give the topsides of the hull the same treatment as the bottom had received the year before: burning off all the old paint, examining the planking, filling the seams and applying seven coats of blue paint to the hull and white boot topping.

We might have known that if one year's workload was light, the next (for 1991) would be troublesome to compensate for it. To start with I found a blister in the new paintwork on the hull which indicated that there was a soft patch in the plank underneath. I could see (a) that the sooner the repair was done the better and (b) that it would be done to a higher standard if I called on Paul Dunbar's shipwrighting skills rather than trying to do it myself. This proved to be a wise decision. Paul's survey showed that the problem had been caused over the years by rainwater blowing in through the cabin porthole and then running down behind a frame, where the trapped water had caused a patch of rot to both frame and planking. The whole problem area could be covered with the palm of one's hand, but Paul, with typical thoroughness required two lengths of hardwood planking each about five feet long in order to space out the scarfed joints to avoid causing any weakness in the hull. The rot damaged frame replacement and an extra one next to it were sawn to shape from greenheart and now my job became to dismantle the cabin furniture (two bunks and the radio equipment cabinet) to give access to the area. Then we found that the frames could not be positioned without cutting away a thick pitchpine stringer, which would later have to be replaced and strengthened. Then we found that one of the new pieces of planking would go beyond the end of the cabin so that part of the wheelhouse structure would have to be removed to reach it. Extra long copper rivets were needed to fasten all this together, with the opportunity being taken to strengthen the pads where the legs bolted through the hull, so that the strength of this vital area was not just repaired, but improved. Altogether over seventy new rivets were put in, a satisfying and enjoyable job for me out on the beach driving them in, but Paul had to suffer the contortions necessary to lie in the restricted space inside to hammer the rivets and roves together.

My turn to suffer came later when many hours of work were needed to reconstruct the radio cabinet, paint the inside of the hull and then replace the bunks and put some new mahogany panelling above them, a process which took all of five week's work. All to cure a blister in the paintwork outside!

Another time consuming and difficult task proved to be the replacement of the main engine propeller shaft and modifications to the stern tube and bearings of the Sabb wing engine, which we ultimately supplied with a new stainless steel shaft as well. Detailing this work would be tedious, but all the work had to be done in very restricted space below the cockpit floorboards putting great strain on the knees and backs of everyone.

The Winter and Christmas passed as we got on with these jobs and as the camellias began to bloom in the garden under the influence of the mild Winter weather, promising good things to come, we were saddened by the death of two of our small, but close, circle of boating friends. On the 9th of January we went to Torquay for the funeral of Joan Leach who kept a flat overlooking the harbour in St Mary's in addition to normally living in the Imperial Hotel at Torquay. She shared our meanderings around the Islands, after losing her husband and giving their motor boat away to the local Nature Conservancy. She had also donated time and wealth into setting up the museum on St Mary's and replacing stained glass windows and woodwork in Old Town Church. She delighted in boating and shrimping and collecting minute shells which she turned into quite spectacular flower pictures. Joan and Peggy became particularly close friends because of the interests they shared together and we all went on a couple of Norwegian coastal steamer holidays together, enjoying the contrast of the ice and snow on the mountains in the Arctic compared with the soft contours and brilliant colours of the Isles of Scilly. Her sudden death left us with a feeling of great loss.

Only two days later we went to the funeral of Harry Hughes who had brought his boat *Havssula* to Scilly many times to share part of our holidays there. Sadly Harry suffered a long illness with cancer which culminated in a brain tumour. We had known him since 1962; we had sailed with him. When he retired from British Airways as a senior flight engineer we helped in finding his ideal retirement home *Pentamar* immediately opposite our house on the Saltash side of the river. Harry took his boat to Spain, Brittany, Ireland, North Wales and finally across the Atlantic to the West Indies and back. In navigation and seamanship he was in a higher league than Peggy and myself, but I am sure he enjoyed nothing better that sharing our enthusiasm and knowledge for pottering around the Isles of Scilly.

The loss of these two good friends came on top of another loss, some while ago, of Derek Pickup. Derek was another addict to the Isles of Scilly. He went there as Manager of Lloyd's Bank in Hugh Street after a distinguished flying career in the R.A.F. in World War II. Before the war he had twinned his love of flying with a love of sailing. After the war was over he found Scilly to be the fulfilment of all his interests. He involved himself happily in all aspects of Island life. He was secretary or treasurer of many Island organisations, he was on the board of the Steamship Company, he was on the Council for a while and he had designed and locally built his dream daysailer for cruising around the Islands and for taking him on his great abiding passion in life: shrimping.

In spite of Lloyd's strict rules about not allowing Bank Managers to stay in one place for more than five years, Derek personally persuaded the top management that he was the right man for Scilly and that he should be allowed to stay. He organised himself a rebuilt cottage at the back of the church, which had views over both the harbour and Porthcressa anchorages. Because of its exposed position it was appropriately called *Windrush*, perhaps with a reference back to his early flying experiences in the 'thirties.

Next to my father, Derek was the strongest influence on my love for sailing, with, in his case a unique love and experience of the Islands to pass on. He also introduced us to the Express Coastal Steamer services around the coast of Norway.

February brought a severe cold spell, damaging the plants in the garden, with extensive sheets of ice floating down the river. Sadly for me such slippery conditions caused a fall while dogwalking in the creek and I damaged three fingers on one hand so badly that work on the boat became impossible for the next three weeks. When I could resume work I rebuilt *Fairwater's* toilet compartment with gleaming mahogany and stainless steel.

On *Fairwater's* last day on our beach, before going out on the mooring and thence on to Scilly, we found that the cabin skylight had been smashed overnight and the boat broken into. The T.V. set, binoculars, some lights and a few other items had been stolen. I had a replacement piece of glass for the skylight in stock, but we had to delay our departure for Scilly until police had been to see the damage and look for fingerprints.

Chapter Seventeen

We did eventually leave the Tamar on Wednesday 18th May for St Mawes and sailed from there to Scilly on the following Saturday. The rest of the month proceeded enjoyably as usual with young great nephew Philip joining us again for the Spring bank holiday week. During his week's stay Philip had the pleasure of enjoying some younger company, because Alba and Roger's son Paul, with girlfriend Anita came down on holiday at the same time and we all met up frequently with the Williams' family in their sailing yacht *Demon de Midi*. Philip received a vary varied range of sailing xperience: he learned how to set the heavy ketch rig on *Fairwater*, enjoyed ailing and (oh bliss!) steering *Demon de Midi* and Roger, with his usual dedication to the young, gave him an intensive crash course on how to sail a 'Topper' dinghy.

In this way we enjoyed the company of the Williams' family every day. t is always a pleasure to see them as they are such close friends. We first met Alba many years ago in Plymouth, when she came to be with Roger who had been rushed into hospital there with a serious head injury, after alling off his cycle on to some granite rocks. The Islands' communication system informed us in Plymouth of this potential tragedy and we met up with Alba to give as much support and encouragement as we could.

Neither of them are native Scillonians but they have fallen for the magic spell of the Islands so intensely that they do not want to live anywhere else. Alba comes from the Bordeaux area in France, of Spanish parentage and her horough training in the business of hotel management was invaluable to her when she was receptionist at Tregarthen's Hotel and still is now when she uns her own bed and breakfast business with great flair and efficiency.

She met Roger in Wales where she was experiencing English hotel work and he was pursuing one of his main interests in life, mountaineering. Roger's athletic abilities, plus his training as a teacher have been invaluable to the sland school. In addition to the usual physical education subjects, Roger has given freely of his time to teach the local children to swim, to canoe and to sail and has taken them skiing on the mountains of Europe and Duke of Edinburgh Award adventures on Dartmoor and numerous camping out expeditions on uninhabited islands in Scilly. A constant bundle of energy, he recovered completely from his accident and has been, above all, a very staunch friend to Peggy and myself.

Their son Paul was an enthusiastic board sailor and racing dinghy helmsman and a natural swimmer, diver and seaman, having been brought up in St Mary's before having to leave for the Mainland to train as an architect. Anita had sailed the Atlantic as a crew member on *Astrid*, an old square rigger. Philip could not have found himself surrounded by a more diverse group of boating enthusiasts and the week made a deep impression on him as he could not wait for any chance to go sailing after returning home to Exmouth.

Soon after he did return, I dislocated my left knee, after a day of staircase varnishing, gardening and finally anchor laying from our dinghy for a large yacht with engine trouble. There were no painful symptoms overnight, but when I got out of my sleeping bag in the morning, the knee dislocated painfully, as had happened several times before, but on this occasion it refused to click back even with a jerk and a push that normally did the trick. The whole leg was useless to put any weight on and produced agony from hip to toe with the slightest movement. I managed to borrow crutches from the local hospital to help me hop around the boat, but at night I could not lie down on the bunk and had to sit up all night, without sleep, while Peggy came to my aid several times with ice packs and hot water bottles to reduce the swelling of the knee and the dogs began to look all sad and sympathetic.

Peggy also had to do all the dogwalking, shopping and dinghy work to the shore and back single handed and of course the weather deteriorated, so we left the harbour for the shelter of Watermill, with Peggy having to do all the anchor work. I had a second sleepless night before we returned to the harbour. Then, in the afternoon, with me not looking forward to a third sleepless night, we became a bit concerned because my foot had become so swollen that we could not get a sock on it, let alone a shoe and the knee, of course, was swollen already. Ted French, a retired surgeon friend of ours had heard from rumours ashore that I was in trouble and after a chat and a look at the leg Peggy rowed him ashore. She returned quite a bit later to say "You won't like this, but we're taking *Fairwater* alongside the quay at nine o'clock tonight and an ambulance is then taking you to the hospital." Ted had diagnosed a probable thrombosis and he knew how essential medical treatment was, because he had suffered a thrombosis himself and had nearly died from a blood clot in his lungs.

That evening I was made comfortable on an adjustable bed, with a cage to keep the bedclothes off the offending leg and with the aid of some pain killers I enjoyed the good night's sleep I so desperately needed. The doctor decided my leg was hopefully not thrombosed after all, but confirmed that had I remained untreated on board *Fairwater* the consequences would have been potentially disastrous. All I had to do now was rest and recover in the beautiful little St Mary's hospital with its views over Porthcressa Bay and receive the attentions of the very friendly and efficient nursing staff.

Peggy, on the other hand, had to face a mountain of problems, which she dealt with swiftly and cheerfully as usual. *Fairwater* had to be left riding to two anchors in the harbour, because no mooring was available and the harbour authorities had to be asked for permission for this because boats should not normally be left at anchor with no one on board. We reluctantly decided that the dogs would have to be sent to Plymouth to ease Peggy's workload, so she took them on *Scillonian III* on Saturday when it poured with rain and blew a southwesterly gale all day, of course. Our good friend Phil collected them from Penzance and drove them back to Plymouth. Another good friend, Tom Chudleigh helped with laying out the second anchor in the harbour.

We had three offers of hospitality for me to recover ashore after my three day stay in hospital and we ended up with two weeks with Alba and Roger in their lovely old granite house in Church Street.

I was being looked after by Dr. Hopwood who was a charming boating type, who kindly resisted the urge to put my badly injured leg in plaster, because he realised that as soon as I could be reasonably mobile, I would want to take *Fairwater* back to the Mainland and a plastered leg would make this impossible. After two weeks I was able to limp on board *Fairwater* from our own dinghy and we were then treated to the luxury of the loan of Tom Chudleigh's mooring in the harbour which removed the anxiety caused by a continuing spell of unsettled weather. Once on board I decided to stay on board for a week rather than risk upsetting my recovery by slipping or falling in the dinghy just to get ashore.

When June turned to July I was able to get ashore daily and do some walking to keep my muscles in trim for the return trip. I was greatly helped in this by Dr. Hopwood, who produced a flexible splint with 'velcro' strapping, which supported the leg while walking, but could be quickly removed for sitting comfortably. How lucky we were to have so many helpful friends and how typical of the Islanders to give unstinting help to anyone in trouble!

On Friday, 5th July, the weather conditions in the morning were quite friendly, but while lunching in the 'Atlantic' an ominous black cloud produced a downpour of rain for a while, clearing away just in time to enable us to return on board in the dry. Then a thunderstorm began to intensify over the Islands, continuing for eight hours, instead of clearing away quickly as usually happens. We heard later that one thunderstorm drifted in from the Mainland while another came from France and the two circled each other right over the Islands. Nobody locally could remember anything like it. Over four inches of rain fell, from skies so black that we had to put the lights on in the cabin all afternoon and evening. A concentrated display of thunder and lightning crashed and flashed all around while the roads ashore turned to rivers and the low lying streets of Hugh Town were flooded. Local radio and T.V. were put out of action, as were the phones, but not before five phone users received shocks, one unfortunate lady being badly burned around her neck and shoulders. Coastguard communication with St Agnes ended when the radio equipment there was hit. The Fire Brigade worked into the early hours of the morning pumping flood water from roads and houses. The electric pumps providing the Islands' water supplies from the bore holes were disabled and the greens of the golf course were scarred and scorched in spite of the downpour of rain. Happily, as far as we know, no boats were hit.

When the storm passed, in the late evening, we found our dinghy half full of rainwater, with floorboards floating at seat level, too full and unstable to climb aboard and having to be bailed with a bucket dropped in on a length of rope. We were grateful that the dogs hadn't been with us for this frightening experience.

On the next day, Saturday, the strong southerly winds which cleared away the thunderstorm caused problems for boats anchored in Porthcressa. A steep swell caused serious problems for two of them. One of them, appropriately named *Swell*, skippered by a sixty seven year old single hander, could not raise its anchor, and the owner had to cut his anchor rope which was snubbing so badly that it was demolishing his stem head. He was obviously a first time visitor because we heard him over the radio asking for directions to find the harbour.

The other incident involved a brand new French catamaran, whose owners had gone ashore for lunch, only to find their boat being smashed up on the rocks between Porthcressa beach and Little Porth. Despite the best efforts of a local salvage boat and the attendance of the Coastguards, the best that could be done was to salvage the mast, gear and furnishings. Two days later the wreck was broken up completely. Built for speed, she had sadly met a quick end.

The strong southeasterlies continued but this did not prevent us taking Roger and Alba afloat for a traditional Sunday day out. We went to New Grimsby for lunch at the New Inn. My knee was now so good that I could walk thirty of forty paces without the aid of a stick and this encouraged me to try some further steps along the road to recovery by putting the outboard on the dinghy and lifting a six gallon can of diesel fuel out of its storage space in the wheelhouse. I did not suffer a twinge of pain in the knee all day, but I might have known that I would have to pay the price for making it work. By bedtime my knee was once more a wobbly, swollen lump of pain, which spread from toe to hip.

It took three days ashore to make me reasonably mobile again, but I was back on board *Fairwater* by Saturday 13th July. As the kettle was warming up for breakfast, we heard a loud bang and clatter from the direction of the quay and our R/T quickly told us that the large mobile crane unloading the local cargo boat *Gry Maritha* had fallen over the edge of the quay, depositing a very heavy container into the sea and giving the crane driver a severe head injury in the process. The local hospital realised that the injured man needed urgent treatment on the Mainland, but by now, fog and drizzle had put an end to all flights from Scilly, so the lifeboat had to be retasked, after returning from a rescue mission with a disabled yacht in tow, to take the casualty to Penzance for ambulance transport to Plymouth.

Scillonian III was doing her demanding double run to the Mainland, but she still found time to use her weight and power to pull the fallen crane back on the quay, showing an impressive display of seamanship by powering astern from the outside of the quay before heading late, but triumphant, back to Penzance again into the evening gloom.

What we did not know was that she was to make a third voyage that night, arriving at two o'clock in the morning to bring over the passengers from the Skybus and Helicopter services who had been unable to fly all day because of the fog. What a day for the crew who had to sail yet again back to the Mainland in the early hours. It is just as well that Scilly observes a travel free day on Sunday (excluding emergencies) so that the crew would have a day to recover.

Both my knee and the weather improved by the following Tuesday, which was a day of perfect calm and sunshine, encouraging us to return to the Mainland next day. While relaxing in the cockpit and soaking up the sunshine, we were delighted to see Rosemary Codd (Co Producer and Director of the videos 'Reflections on Scilly' and 'The Islander') paddling around in her new canoe *Salamander* and she bravely climbed aboard from the canoe to join us for a drink.

Next morning we returned, in calm weather, to the Helford, where we were able to shelter from a southwesterly gale, before returning to our mooring in the Tamar on Sunday, 21st July. With the aid of my walking stick I was able to climb up the steps from the quay to our house, where we were given a very restrained welcome from Skip and Ike who had not forgiven us for sending them home early. With the aid of the same walking stick I was able to give young Philip a fortnight's cruise to Fowey and Falmouth in early August, to complete a fairly eventful boating season 1991.

Having been retired now for seven years, the annual trips to Scilly were becoming an enjoyable routine. This year *Fairwater* needed only one major repair, an area of decking over the galley having begun to go soft because of rainwater leaking under the extractor fan housing. We decided that if I could get a crew, Peggy would stay at home with the dogs until *Fairwater* reached Scilly and then bring the dogs over on *Scillonian III* because their sealegs were stiffening with age and a long, rough sea passage would be cruel to them. Nobody showed any compassion for me, in my sixty second year, so it was taken for granted that I could cope with such problems.

The perfect crew emerged in the form of Bob Hosking, a good friend of many years' standing, a boat surveyor, boatbuilder, boat designer, sailing addict and experienced seaman. We first met him when he married Janice, the teenage crew who had sailed with us in *Vyaj* back in the sixties. She would come down with Peggy and the dogs and spend a week or so with us on *Fairwater* before their work commitments called them back to Plymouth again.

Bob and I arrived in Scilly on May 19th and Peggy, Janice and the dogs arrived on the *Scillonian* at lunchtime next day. The normal idyllic Scillonian holiday followed, taking friends with us on trips around the Islands nearly every day, while the weather remained kind for the next month and we enjoyed the very welcome bonus of being able to use Tom Chudleigh's mooring in the harbour which he was unable to use while going through a patch of bad health.

Peggy and the dogs returned on the *Scillonian* on Saturday, 4th July, while Bob came over on the return trip to act as faithful crew for the cruise back to Plymouth, which we enjoyed for a week, calling in at the usual ports on the way home.

In August I took young Philip for a fortnight's 'minicruise' along the coast to the Helford, where he sailed, outboarded and swam to his heart's content, now being a very competent, agile and cheerful crew. The usual daytrips to Plymouth Sound and up the river Tamar brought the boating season to an end by the last day of October.

Chapter Eighteen

1993

When *Fairwater* was laid up in the Autumn of '92 she was in such good condition that no deck or planking repair work was necessary, so the Winter could be devoted to much needed dinghy repair work.

When the Winter cover was lashed down and the masts were removed we took the old mizzen sail to John McKillop's sail loft at Kingsbridge, to have it replaced by a new fifteen per cent larger one, which would make full use of a new spruce boom which I had made earlier in '92.

The first dinghy given full restoration treatment was our treasured Fairey Marine 'Dinky' which had been towed from Plymouth to Scilly and back over the past three decades. The original rubber fender was removed, as were the layers of varnish accumulated over the last forty years, for light mahogany staining and seven coats of 'Blue Peter' varnish to produce a surprisingly good finish.

The dinghy was then turned the right way up and the real work began. The old rowlock plates, which had rusted and begun to rot the woodwork were removed and new hardwood pads were shaped and jointed into the sound wood to take new replacements. The old floorboards were scrapped as they were falling apart and replaced with hardwood strips, of similar shape to the old battens, which were bonded to the original hull material to add extra strength. Finally a new, larger white rubber fender replaced the old one and by mid December the refit was complete with a gleaming 'Fairey' ready for action.

Next, our fourteen feet Norwegian 'With' dinghy was given an equally thorough refit as the first months of 1993 came along. After all this hard, but enjoyable work, the routine fitting out loomed ahead and Peggy and I had to sit down and think about what the future held for a couple now in their mid sixties, with dogs rapidly approaching old age. We surveyed our financial resources and decided that we could cash in shares and building society savings sufficient to buy a modest home ashore on St Mary's which we could enjoy when we were no longer fit enough to enjoy our holiday 'home afloat', which was so demanding in bad weather. Prices of freehold property in the Islands are about double the equivalent on the Mainland and we had never been able before to aspire to become Island property owners. By turning our savings into a home ashore, we could then, in due course sell *Fairwater* and save ourselves all the expense and trouble of maintaining such an old wooden boat, making financial sense out of our change of lifestyle. With a suitable small boat we could still enjoy inter-island trips in Summer and with a permanent home ashore we could enjoy Scilly all the year around, if we so wished. So the final link between Tamar and Scilly could be forged with a home in each.

So much for the theory; now down to the practicalities. Firstly a list from the local Estate Agent and then twist the arms of our good friends Roger and Alba to look at the possibilities. By late January we were able to fly down by Skybus to look at four possibilities, only one of which proved to be worth having professionally surveyed. It had views over the harbour, was close to all the facilities of Hugh Town but was a self catering let property which would have taken a lot of work to convert into an acceptable home ashore. After the survey we put in a reasonable offer for it, which, thankfully, was not accepted and by the end of February we heard from the Estate Agent that another suitable property had just been put on the market, so we came down for another daytrip by helicopter to look at *Lower Ganilly*.

This was a freehold flat, just a hundred yards from Porthmellon Beach, within easy walking distance of all the shops, the pubs and the tripper boat facilities on the quay. Within a few days we negotiated a deal with the owners and the only delay was caused by the technical difficulties of buying a 'split freehold'. Our excellent solicitor in Plymouth sorted these out so that we became the proud owners of *Lower Ganilly* on June 4th.

Of course we wanted to take *Fairwater* to Scilly as usual in May and there were three advantages in doing so. Firstly we could enjoy our usual boating activities when the weather was good enough to tempt us away from furnishing and decorating the flat; secondly we would have a home afloat to give us plenty of time to prepare the flat and thirdly we could transport down from Plymouth some furniture and furnishings which would be impossible to buy from the limited shopping facilities in St Mary's.

We postponed our departure date from May 10th to May 24th because of a delay in the completion date resulting from the legal complications. As this period of delay brought a lot of wet and windy weather we did not consider that we lost much. It also gave me time to convert two thirds of *Fairwater's* spacious main cabin into a cargo hold with safe stowage for items if we met with rough weather. This resulted in reducing the sleeping accommodation there to one bunk, although we could still use part of the cabin table for mealtimes. Bob Hosking agreed to be crew for the trip down as last year and as he enjoyed sleeping in the cosy fo'c'sle bunk anyway, *Fairwater's* conversion to cargo carrying would be no problem. Also as last year, Peggy, the dogs and Bob's wife Janice could come over on *Scillonian III* and live on board as soon as we had arrived and ferried the cargo ashore, reconverting *Fairwater's* accommodation to its normal layout. This may sound complicated, but it was in fact far simpler than packing everything for delivery to Penzance, shipping it across to St Mary's and finding stowage for it ashore until such time as we could take over the flat.

Bob was able to complete his business commitments two days earlier than expected, so we were finally able to leave the Tamar on Saturday, May 22nd. The cargo included a new vacuum cleaner, new bedding and kitchenware and even a lawn mower, a total of fifteen packages of assorted sizes. With full water and fuel tanks and our usual cruising gear and provisions, *Fairwater's* white line dipped gently into the sea, instead of floating several inches above it.

A southeasterly force four with patches of drizzle was forecast and although this direction is favourable for voyaging down channel, we anticipated some steep seas off the headlands. The worst of these, in the event, were off Penlee Point and Rame Head but by slowing to five knots and holding on tightly *Fairwater's* seaworthy hull took us safely out to sea until we could turn down channel and run before the seas in the direction of Fowey.

The next day was less windy and still with the favouring easterly direction. This took us pleasantly to St Mawes for the night. The evening brought heavy cloud and rain and from two a.m. onwards we had a succession of thunderstorms, with heavy downpours of rain.

This was not very encouraging for taking on the long trip to Scilly next day, but we raised anchor in yet another deluge of heavy rain and set out into the murk, quite prepared to run into the Helford river if conditions did not improve. The lightning overnight had knocked out Radio Cornwall's FM transmitters, so our usual local weather information was not available. We did, however, find a crackling transmission on medium wave with a forecast of southeasterlies, force three to four, becoming cyclonic three to four with thunderstorms at times. We could cope with bad visibility in the rain, thanks to the accuracy of our Decca Navigator so we decided to head on for the Lizard, which we sighted in improving visibility at eleven o'clock and then headed for Scilly. Although the higher parts of the Cornish coastline were still hidden in fog, visibility at sea level improved all the time, so we were able to see the Islands from ten miles off by mid afternoon and as we came in through Crow Sound the blazing Scillonian sun broke through. Warm greetings came from our friends ashore and Tom Chudleigh was particularly helpful in storing a lot of our cargo in his boatyard until we could get possession of *Lower Ganilly*.

An evening meal at the Atlantic Inn celebrated the safe arrival of ship, crew and cargo in much better than average time.

On the next day we had to unload all the cargo and remove the stowage battens, or there would have been no bunk for Peggy to sleep in on her arrival the day after. The southeasterly wind brought sheltered conditions to the harbour which was helpful but the rain it brought with it meant that every package had to be wrapped in a bin liner for the journey ashore in our little dinghy. Peggy, Janice and the dogs arrived on schedule on Wednesday, though Janice suffered an Achilles heel injury through having to sprint to catch the *Scillonian* after parking difficulties with her car.

Bob and Janice stayed on board with us for a week and we all enjoyed the usual day trips and dogwalks. We also enjoyed the luxury of using Tom Chudleigh's mooring instead of anchoring, especially when we had a gale one night which blew a French yacht ashore on the rocks of Newford Island and caused quite a number of other yachts to drag their anchors, colliding with their neighbours in the rain and the darkness.

Just three days later we were given the keys of *Lower Ganilly* so our boating activities were curtailed while we did what little decorating was necessary, organized some new carpets and unpacked the fifteen boxes of cargo stowed ashore. We still lived on *Fairwater*, while we waited for beds, wardrobes, bedside tables, bedding, curtains and lampshades etcetera to arrive on the cargo boat *Gry Maritha* from Penzance, where we bought these items from a firm offering free delivery to St Mary's quay as part of the deal. We loved our new flat, with its garden overlooking the anchorage off Porthmellon Beach. Nothing was needed for the kitchen, which was larger and better equipped than the one in our home at Plymouth, other than a washing machine which was installed by the local electrical dealer, yes, St Mary's does have one of those! The bathroom and separate toilet were spacious and in immaculate condition; how we thanked our lucky stars that our first choice with all its staircases, small rooms and dilapidated decoration had come to nothing. We selected the furniture for the dining/sitting room from stores in Plymouth, choosing flatpack items wherever possible to make transport easy. We had great fun choosing and buying these items, now that we could easily afford them, in comparison with the difficulties of setting up our first home when we were young and impoverished.

Also we realized how lucky we were to have *Fairwater* as a floating home while we were furnishing the flat, rather than having to live out of suitcases in hotel accommodation which is what most people would have to do. Some of our love for Scilly seemed to help us set up such a cheerful, informal and comfortable home there. The owners of the freehold flat upstairs, Gib and Pauline Pender, were kindness itself, contributing to the feeling of happiness we found there.

Mid to late June brought wet and unsettled weather which was just right for painting and decorating rather than boating. The carpet layers finished by the end of June and the sitting/dining room furniture arrived shortly afterwards to be assembled. Wherever we could we used natural pine and cane furniture to give a warm, but informal feel to the flat.

By the end of June the flat was sufficiently completed to enable us to invite friends there for meals and for the first two weeks of July we shared our time between the boat and the new flat with all our Island friends taking an interest in how our home ashore was progressing. We could now look forward to years of enjoying a base both in Scilly and on the Tamar. We could look forward to Scilly in the Autumn, the Winter and the early Spring, which would be a new experience for us. *Lower Ganilly* had enough rooms to bring my mother down to stay or other friends and relatives when she was not there.

We never know what surprises life holds for us. Little did I think that in less than three years my lifestyle would be turned upside down, that *Fairwater* after thirty three years of ownership would disappear from my life and that I would end up living permanently, alone, on St Mary's.

Meanwhile, Saturday July 10th arrived and so did Bob Hosking on the *Scillonian*, to crew *Fairwater* back to the Mainland with me. This we did over the next three days, calling in to the river Helford and Fowey on the way.

Before picking up a mooring in Fowey, Bob and I anchored off Portmellon, near Mevagissey, where *Fairwater* had been built. Bob had to do a quick survey on a teak built Eventide yacht laid up ashore there and while he was doing this I was able to visit Percy Mitchell's widow. Percy had built *Fairwater* in 1930 and his widow could remember how the design work had been done on the kitchen table, after the evening meal, when Percy had already done a long and hard day's work. The very pleasant house she lived in, overlooking the site of the boatyard (now defunct) and the bay was in fact originally a lifeboat house, where *Fairwater* was stored for the duration of World War II. She was delighted to remember old times and talk about her remarkably gifted boatbuilder husband, who she had obviously adored.

Then we went on across St Austell Bay in perfect Summer weather, to Fowey, picking up the last available swinging mooring for the night. Next morning we had a dreary uncomfortable passage back to the Tamar, rolling about in steep seas and poor visibility in a strong southwesterly wind. We did pick up the mooring at 12:30, becoming thoroughly soaked in a downpour of rain while sorting out the mooring ropes which had become muddy and weed covered over the seven weeks we had been away.

This did not mean the end of the boating season for 1993. Fired with enthusiasm for completing the furnishing of the flat, we decided to give *Fairwater* a quick refit on the beach, convert her again into a cargo carrier and fill her once more with furniture, furnishings, power tools, garden tools and assorted domestic equipment which in the end totalled twenty seven packages, piled up so high that the cane chairs which formed the top layer were jammed against the deck beams, ensuring that the pile of cargo was not going to move while at sea.

Young Philip arrived once more to act as crew, torn between the excitement of seeing the new flat in Scilly for the first time and his hopes that the journey down would take as long as possible so that he could enjoy boating and sailing (in hired dinghies) as frequently as possible on the way down channel. We did in fact take a week before arriving in St Mary's on Friday 30th July. Philip sailed a Mirror dinghy at Fowey (in the rain) a Topper and then a Laser and finally a high speed outboard dory in the Helford. This together with using our dinghy with its Suzuki outboard and some rowing just about managed to satisfy his enthusiasm and routine fishing and swimming from *Fairwater* completed the programme nicely.

While we were travelling down by sea, the 'shore party' who were going to stay in the flat prepared to travel down by road to Penzance and then by *Scillonian III* to St Mary's. The 'shore-party' consisted of Peggy and the two dogs, my ninety one year old mother and a good friend and neighbour of ours 'Pic' Baigent, who loves boating and the Scillies and who happens to be a needlewoman, very happy to help with the curtains, bedding and anything else that came along. Philip and I would sleep on board *Fairwater* enjoy the meals and activity ashore on some days and take Peggy and Pic out boating when they could spare the time. In this way, everybody was happy to spend a week or so before Philip and I headed back up channel in *Fairwater*, while the 'shore-party' could stay on for a couple more weeks after that.

When we did arrive in Scilly in the late afternoon we were suffering from rough sea conditions for the second half of the trip as the northwesterly wind came straight at us off the Atlantic, reaching its forecast force five to six. From Wolf Rock lighthouse onwards I had to remain at the wheel and reduce speed to prevent any breaking seas coming on board. Philip was tired and went below to sleep on his bunk in the fo'c'sle, but after seeing his cabin portholes frequently going under water as *Fairwater's* bow plunged into the deep green seas, he decided to retire to the main cabin, from which it would be easier to escape if we nosedived into the sea and did not come up again!

Porthcressa was sheltered from the northwest so we anchored there rather than in the harbour. The violent motion caused the topping lift of our mizzen sail to break and when we lowered the sail, the boom, sheets and sail all clattered down into an untidy heap on the cockpit floor. We took the sail off the boom, disconnected the boom from its broken mast fitting and lashed it down on deck out of the way, tidying up the halliard and broken topping lift as best we could.

We then took the dinghy ashore, which must have looked strange to people on the beach, as our little eight foot dinghy had two large cane armchairs and a large bag of bedding piled up between us, making visibility difficult when steering the outboard from the stern. After carrying this load to the flat with some difficulty we reported our safe arrival to our respective homes, had a celebratory evening meal ashore and slept soundly until three o'clock in the morning when the wind went from northwest to southwest, sending some uncomfortable sea into the anchorage. We consequently moved after breakfast to St Mary's harbour which would be better sheltered according to the morning forecast and which would also be much closer to the flat for unloading cargo.

We prepared to anchor in our usual spot, but we noticed that Tom Chudleigh's mooring was unoccupied so we made a swift change of plan and picked up Tom's mooring before going ashore to ask for permission to use it. We loaded the dinghy again with an assortment of boxes and bags, with barely room enough left for the crew and headed for the Rechabite Slip. There we could see Tom, who turned his back on us and purposefully strode back to his yard. I feared that we had upset him by picking up his mooring before we had found time to ask permission. How pleased we were, therefore, to see him stride purposefully back towards us, as we approached in our heavily laden dinghy, wheeling his handcart down the slip, to help with our unloading. After friendly greetings and handshakes I asked him:

"Is it alright if we use your mooring?"

"Course you can" was the immediate reply. This gave us a secure base for *Fairwater*, as close as possible to *Lower Ganilly*.

I spent many hours at the flat, unpacking our boxes and assembling flatpacked furniture, while Philip enjoyed pushing Tom's wooden handcart up from the beach. Yet again I was thrilled by this apparent timewarp away from modern life's heartlessly efficient mechanical life style to the slower, happier pace of Cornish holidays remembered from decades ago.

Within three days of our arrival the flat was fit for occupation, the furniture in place and the bedding expertly laid in place by Philip, who, characteristically had helped his mother at home with such domestic chores, while she was busy carving out a career for herself as a Bank Manager, as well as being a mother and housewife.

On Monday, August 2nd, Peggy, Pic, the dogs and my mother in her wheelchair all arrived on the *Scillonian* after a voyage in gentle breezes, blue skies and bright sunshine. This was a dramatic improvement on the weather conditions in the early hours of the morning, when we had watched the salvage, in a downpour of rain, of an unattended yacht that had blown ashore on Newford Island. Such is the swiftly changing weather pattern caused by Scilly's isolated position in the Atlantic.

Philip and I continued our boating, fishing and shrimping activities while sleeping on *Fairwater*, while Peggy and Pic took turns in looking after my mother ashore and enjoying days afloat with us. One problem we did have to sort out on *Fairwater* was a cooling problem with the Sabb diesel. We put *Fairwater* ashore at Old Grimsby to check that the seawater intake was clear and the ubiquitous Philip, working in very restricted space in the bilge took the cooling water pump apart and discovered at the third attempt that we had a split diaphragm, which we could replace with a spare that we carried on board.

I was very relieved that this problem was solved, because we had now been in Scilly for a week and it was time to head for home, for which full mechanical efficiency was essential. We did in fact return to the Helford on Sunday and after a brief spell of bad weather returned home to the Tamar on the following Tuesday. Philip was anxious to return to his new home in Exmouth, while *Fairwater* was brought back onto our beach for a brief refit. The 'shore-party' at *Lower Ganilly* arrived back a week later and before the year ended we returned by the *Scillonian* to stay at the flat, fitting new varnished doors and replacing an old garden shed with a purpose built workshop, for which a strong workbench was built in Plymouth before being taken apart to travel to Penzance and then to St Mary's, with Phil helping with all this activity and travelling down with me for a couple of weeks in November to erect the shed and fit the new doors.

By the end of the year we had used the flat for fourteen weeks, we had worked hard on it and we were delighted with it, not least because it would be our foothold ashore in Scilly, when advancing years, both of boat and ourselves, made the voyages down from the Tamar too difficult to cope with.

Chapter Nineteen

1994

1993 had been the peak year both for our boating activities (with two trips to Scilly instead of our usual one) and the very enjoyable process of buying, furnishing and using our flat at the bottom of Jackson's Hill, St Mary's. As frequently happens in life, a peak is naturally followed by a trough. One omen of this was the weather during the Winter of '93/'94. It proved to be the wettest Winter in Britain since records began. Then February brought frost and snow on a scale most unusual for the South West of England.

The weather may have had something to do with the state of health of our two dogs, who were now in their fifteenth year. Skip worried us most, having a severe intestinal infection which gave him great discomfort, rapid loss of weight (and even appetite!) necessitating a couple of urgent visits to the Vet. On each occasion we said our goodbyes to him as we drove him to the veterinary hospital. On each occasion, after treatment he made an amazing recovery, looking for his regular dogwalk next morning. He had an operation just before Christmas and then survived into the New Year when every week became a bonus for us, as, "living on borrowed time" to use the Vet's words, he gradually regained his old enjoyment of life, even though his former agility had gone for good.

My agility was also beginning to suffer as I reached my sixty fourth year and Peggy had to cope with an arthritis problem in her knees which made climbing in and out of our little eight foot dinghy a problem, as well as having to drag it up and down the long sandy beaches of Scilly. The only solution I could see was to acquire a larger inflatable to replace our eight foot Avon which would be lighter, more stable and safer than the wooden 'Fairey'. I searched the adverts in the Western Morning News for weeks, looking for a nine or ten foot inflatable with a wooden transom, without success.

Then I asked the boatyard in Salcombe, where we had always gone for our Suzuki outboard engines, if they happened to have anything suitable in their second-hand sales list and we had a phone call back to say they could offer a choice of two twelve foot six Zodiac inflatables, both of which were in 'as new' condition. Moving up from eight feet to twelve feet six in length means doubling the weight so that stowage of such a large inflatable on

Fairwater's deck would become a problem. But it would mean doubling the stability and carrying capacity and its safety aspect also appealed because it was in reality a slightly smaller version of the R.N.L.I. inshore lifeboats. The next thing to do was obviously to go to Salcombe and look at the monsters.

There was no difficulty in making the choice: they both had strong wooden transoms which would take either one powerful outboard, or two smaller ones, but one of them had a gleaming stainless steel unit with four rubber wheels, which could be lowered for pulling it up or down beaches and which could then be raised when under way. I negotiated a part exchange deal for the old Avon dinghy and our Johnson 4HP outboard and we became the proud new owners of our Zodiac on the spot. We actually brought it back home with us on the roofrack of the car and by mid February it started its working life, being rowed and motored around by young Philip and my godson David Hendy, when they came to spend their half term holiday with us. I adapted the transom so that it would take two Suzuki 2HP outboards. The advantages of this arrangement, rather than using one larger engine were firstly the added safety of having an extra engine in case of mechanical trouble with the other one and secondly these very lightweight small engines would be easy for me to carry over the hundred yards or so from the flat to Porthmellon beach on St Mary's where I intended to keep her.

We already had one practically new Suzuki so the purchase of another from the same firm supplying the new inflatable completed the new rig. We were delighted with its stability, lightness and seaworthiness so now it deserved a name. I suggested she should be called *MOBIRD* and after looking puzzled Peggy and the boys happily approved of the new name which was a mnemonic for "My Own Bloody Inflatable Rescue Dinghy".

As the year progressed, I went to stay at the flat in late February, sending over two heavy toolboxes and the workbench on *Gry Maritha*, while Phil arrived later by air to help me with the fitting out of the new workshop and installing an electrical supply. While this was going on, Peggy stayed at home, looking after the dogs, who both went through a patch of bad health. It was only fair that when I returned I could look after the house and dogs while Peggy could go to the flat for some rest and recuperation and do a bit of Spring cleaning as well.

It was now high time to fit out *Fairwater* for her next "cargo run" to Scilly which we hoped to time as usual for the middle of May. By the end of the first week in May *Fairwater* was afloat on her mooring, with an assortment of furniture, pictures and kitchen equipment and by way of a change from the previous year, eighteen standard bay bushes (which I had grown myself as a hobby) and eighteen variegated leaved geraniums and six wooden plant troughs to grow them in. The idea of the plant troughs was, at three feet long, they could hold down the plastic 'fun grass' which would cover Gib's concrete garage roof and make it look more like an extension of our garden.

Coinciding with *Fairwater's* use as a cargo carrier and also to reduce windage when at anchor in Porthmellon, I decided to leave the mainmast and its rigging ashore in Plymouth, reducing the sail area to the new mizzen rig we set up last year. Tom Chudleigh had now finished building his fishing boat, so his mooring would not be available. The mizzen would be a useful steadying sail when at sea and the removal of the mast, boom and rigging gave *Fairwater* a large expanse of uncluttered deck space, a really useful storage area, as we found on the journey down.

I slept on board *Fairwater* for security reasons, remembering that once before we had been burgled on the eve of departure. The wooden 'Fairey' dinghy was lashed down on the deck and the much larger inflatable would take her previous place, being towed astern. A favourable weather forecast, several days before we were due to leave encouraged me to make some progress down channel single handed, an interesting and challenging proposition, as I had never taken *Fairwater* any distance before without the assistance of a crew. Again Peggy and the dogs, my mother and Janice would make their way to the flat on *Scillonian III*, while Bob would join me somewhere along the coast to act as crew for the crossing to Scilly.

Bob did in fact join me, when his business commitments permitted, at St Mawes. Only one small hitch occurred in all these arrangements. After towing *Mobird* astern to St Mawes, I found she had three or four buckets of seawater in her and as we had enjoyed a flat calm passage, this could not be caused by spray, but proved she must have a small leak somewhere. This was no great problem thus far, but could prove to be quite a big problem if we hit rough water on the much longer passage to Scilly.

The answer to this problem was to stow *Mobird* on deck and tow the 'Fairey' astern as usual. Bob and I used the mizzen halliard to lower the 'Fairey' over the side and then lift *Mobird* on board in its place. As *Mobird* was twice the size of the 'Fairey' there was some difficulty in stowing it on deck. Previously, after some measurement, I had decided that it was an impossibility. What I had forgotten was that, by partial deflation, it could be pushed and lashed into a smaller area and although it was not altogether a pretty sight, this is what we did, to our considerable satisfaction, in spite of having to struggle for about an hour in the pouring rain. The crew were revived by a couple of glasses of Scotch, followed by a hot and filling Ship's Beef Stew. Bob stowed his gear in the fo'c'sle and settled into his familiar bunk and we both slept well while the rain continued to drum on the deck and the southeasterly wind increased, causing no problems in our sheltered anchorage at St Mawes.

The next early morning shipping forecast told of winds strengthening to gale force, so the crew snuggled down in warm sleeping bags and went back to sleep again, to breakfast at a more civilised time. It was not until Sunday May 15th that the weather improved enough for us to take our heavily laden *Fairwater* to Scilly. By then Peggy, the dogs and Bob's wife Janice had arrived at the flat, travelling on *Scillonian III* as usual and had spent a couple of days settling in. We agreed that I would sleep ashore, while Bob and Janice slept on *Fairwater* where they would have the use of the 'Fairey' dinghy while I kept *Mobird* on her wheels at the top of Porthmellon beach. These wheels had already demonstrated their usefulness, because we could fill *Mobird* with cargo and then push her, like a wheelbarrow, all the way up the beach and then along the road to the entrance to the flat.

A week later, Bob and Janice returned to the Mainland and the 'Fairey' dinghy was stowed in the garden of the flat, while *Mobird* took over the dinghy work from our corner of Porthmellon beach. The month of June arrived and passed, with an enjoyable mixture of holidaying ashore and afloat. For the first months of our stay we also enjoyed the luxury of using Tom Chudleigh's mooring, as his new fishing boat was in the final stages of completion, before going on the mooring itself. The launch of Tom's boat was an interesting operation as it had to be lifted over the high granite wall of his boatyard because it was too big to go through the gateway. With no mobile crane on the island, this had to be done with two lorries using their hydraulic loading gear. With typical Scillonian ingenuity this was achieved with one lorry then carrying the boat down the slipway to the beach, where the other one then lifted it off onto the sand, all without a scratch on the gleaming new paintwork.

Our Summer idyll continued as in previous years: living in the flat, boat trips in *Fairwater*, socialising with our Island friends and enjoying a week's visit from our niece Jacki.

We had agreed to let the flat to some friends from July 11th, so Peggy with the shore party went back to Plymouth a few days beforehand, while I waited a few more days for young Philip to arrive to act as crew for the voyage home.

As I walked the dogs around the lifeboat house path and down to the quay, our black and white Springer, Ike, moved ever more slowly and finally stopped walking altogether. He was suffering from old age and in addition, I think his doggy intuition told him that this would be his last visit to Scilly, so he decided that he just didn't want to go home. The departure time for the *Scillonian* was now only a few minutes away. I tied Skip to the first iron mooring ring I could find on the quay and carried the motionless Ike in my arms, sixty pounds of deadweight dog, hurrying as fast as I could. A worried Peggy came back down the gangway realising that something was amiss to make me so late and the sight of poor old Ike in my arms explained everything. Peggy dashed back along the quay to collect Skip, while Ike and I leaned against the wall and tried to recuperate.

This was an ill omen that our Summer idyll was over and in fact, two events were shortly to cast a shadow over our lives: Skip suffered a stroke soon after arriving home and more ominously, although unknown to me at the time, Peggy had already organised an appointment with her doctor, because she found that she had a lump in her breast.

Peggy had intended to keep this bad news to herself until Philip and I were safely home, but events moved too quickly for that. Within a few days, thanks to our health insurance policy, Peggy had seen a consultant in the Nuffield hospital in Plymouth and as he found the lump was malignant, he arranged for the necessary surgery to take place just a few days later.

On hearing this news over the 'phone Philip and I now had to get home as quickly as possible, so, of course, the weather turned nasty with forecasts of strong southeasterly headwinds. As if this was not bad enough, even *Fairwater* seemed to be in for a spell of bad luck, because as we rolled at anchor in the unsettled weather a loud metallic clanging noise came from our rudder, which could only be caused by a very badly worn bottom bearing. Just when I needed to get home quickly, I had to face up to the fact that *Fairwater* had to be taken ashore for repair. If I took the easy option of setting off up channel and just hope for the best, I could see a series of disasters lying in wait. The chances were that we would set off in unfavourable weather conditions. With the boat pitching and rolling, with frequent effort needed on the steering wheel to meet steep seas head on, the bottom bearing of the rudder would fail and the steering would not work. With the responsibility I had for the safety of my young nephew on board I would have to send out a 'Mayday' call for lifeboat assistance. Until that arrived *Fairwater* could go broadside on to the seas, the wheelhouse windows could be smashed and the open cockpit could be flooded, putting us in ever increasing likelihood of being swamped and sunk.

This was the last thing Peggy needed as she prepared to go into hospital for surgery. She already had Skip so badly affected by a stroke that he could only get out into the garden by being supported with a towel under his tummy to take the weight off his staggering paws. The Vet was optimistic that he would recover, so it would not be easy to have him put to sleep.

I talked the rudder problem over with Tom Chudleigh who agreed that any risk taking was out of the question.

"You can put her in on my beach moorings" my good friend said, "and we'll check them over this afternoon to make sure they are O.K"

That evening *Fairwater* came into the beach in the most sheltered part of the harbour in warm evening sunshine, where we enjoyed the bliss of flat calm, compared with rolling in the exposed part of the harbour. This made for a much needed good night's sleep, after I took a number of photos to record the scene where *Fairwater* had never actually been before, in all her thirty one visits.

Next morning, when the tide went out I was able to inspect the bearing, fortunately with the assistance of our friend from Plymouth who was a marine engineer. We found there was an eighth of an inch wear all around the bearing, meaning that the heavy rudder could swing a quarter of an inch each way every time the boat rolled. The good news was that there was still three quarters of the iron pin left which would make it reasonably safe on the way home.

One of the retired tripper boat skippers strolled past and had a look at it and said

"It'll get you home, but it won't stop you worrying."

This made up my mind. If the nearby Scillonian Steamship workshop could cut off the old pin and weld on a new one, the whole problem would be solved. The engineer in charge there was an old friend and although he was going on holiday next day and could not find the time to do the job himself he said that if we could remove the rudder ourselves and bring it to the workshop, he would phone for a welder to come straight away to deal with it.

So, again, the helpful spirit of the Islanders came to the rescue of someone in trouble. Philip and I unbolted the rudder and just about managed to carry it between us across the beach to the workshop. The welder cut off the old pin, found a correctly sized piece of new iron rod to replace it and with great skill and patience welded the new item into place. An hour later we were carrying the rudder back down the beach as fast as we could to bolt it back in position before the tide came in again.

The whole job, which would have been difficult and expensive to have done back in Plymouth cost me less than ten pounds when I went into the chandlery to pay the bill next morning! I would gladly have paid several hundreds for the peace of mind this repair gave me.

As the easterly headwinds continued we waited a few more days before heading home, even then having a very rough trip of over eleven hours to reach St Mawes. I was by now so anxious, so tired and so stressed that I decided that although the old boat could take the strain of such voyages, I was getting too old to enjoy it any longer. My depressed mood lightened next day when we moved on to Fowey in ideal sunny conditions, with a gentle northwesterly wind, which would have been ideal for the trip back from Scilly compared with the day before.

We were back on our mooring on Wednesday 20th July, with just one day to spare before Peggy went into hospital. But we were safely back, though not in the most cheerful of circumstances. Skip was much improved, but it was sad to see his staggering attempt at a welcome home to *Fairwater's* crew.

While Peggy was in hospital for five days and then over the next few weeks of recuperation, *Fairwater* was brought onto the beach for a mid season refit. One reason for this was that I had put her on the market for sale through the 'Wooden Ships' brokerage and we wanted to make her as presentable as possible for any prospective purchaser.

Apart from a few day trips, *Fairwater* only had one weekend cruise to Fowey and back with my godson David Hendy and his father as crew. Then Peggy began five weeks of daily radiotherapy treatment, so *Fairwater* naturally spent most of that time on the mooring.

On each day of treatment I walked the dogs in the local park next to the cancer clinic, which had a view out over Plymouth Sound. Our now very elderly dogs walked so slowly over the grassy slopes, but they always recognised Peggy from a distance as she returned after her treatment and while they wagged their tails enthusiastically in greeting, Peggy would give them her big, confident smile. All through the hospitalization and the weeks of treatment afterwards Peggy never indulged herself in self pity but, on the contrary, always told sympathetic friends, neighbours and relatives that she had just had a little operation followed by some painless radiotherapy and that nobody should be over fearful or embarrassed about discussing the word 'cancer', which so many people naturally dreaded.

In spite of this optimistic mood, we could not deny that our lives had changed drastically and swiftly. Our boat, which had been our lifeline to the Isles of Scilly was for sale. Our dogs were "on their last legs" as the stiffness and slowness of old age overtook them. Their Winter walks became painfully slow so we bought them a couple of smart Barbour dog coats to keep out the cold and the rain and they had to be lifted into the back of our Citroën estate car as they could no longer jump up into it unaided.

But we still had our holiday home ashore on Scilly and this was a haven of happiness which we could still visit and take friends and relatives with us over the Winter and Spring, while looking forward to the next Summer, with our Zodiac inflatable on the beach, ready to take us around our beloved Off Islands as in years gone by.

Chapter Twenty

1995 onwards

This year brought the final parting with *Fairwater*. Not as bad an experience as losing a friend or a dog to the finality of death, because a new life existed for the boat under new ownership. It was still sad to part with a loyal servant after over three decades of service.

Peggy had been down to *Lower Ganilly* for a couple of weeks recuperation and celebration of the end of her radiotherapy treatment in October and I went down to do a few maintenance jobs on the flat and the boats in November to prepare them for the onset of Winter.

We made visits again in April and May, but for the first time *Fairwater* was left behind in Plymouth instead of heading for Scilly in the middle of May. We put *Fairwater* up for sale in the hands of the brokerage at Clovelly Bay Marina at Turnchapel. As part of the deal we were given free berthing at the marina, where prospective purchasers could be shown over her, while we were holidaying at the flat.

Our inflatable dinghy *Mobird* with its two Suzuki outboards took us around the Islands very efficiently although Peggy's back suffered from the bouncing and the buffeting inevitable with an inflatable if the wind rose over force 4 and stirred up choppy sea conditions. We returned to the Mainland at the end of July.

Apart from the fact that this was our routine date for ending our Summer holiday, I had to get back to Plymouth because I had entered *Fairwater* in the '95 Classic Boat Rally, based in the marina at Turnchapel, partly as a gesture of thanks to the marina for its generous hospitality and partly because there might be, among the numerous spectators, a prospective puchaser who could see *Fairwater* under way. The old boat looked very smart with her traditional lines and we took pride in the fact that only about ten per cent of the entries were any older.

Meanwhile *Mobird* had taken us around the Islands very efficiently on exploratory daytrips in addition to the old familiar ones and we enjoyed a couple of shrimping expeditions and took our niece Jacki out frequently when she came to visit us for a fortnight in the middle of June.

We enjoyed the participation in the 'Classic Rally' at Turnchapel Marina where the local pubs provided jazzy music in the evenings, but no serious buyer appeared as a result of the experience. As the sailing season was drawing to a close and I was not looking forward to fitting *Fairwater* out again in the following Spring, I decided to drop the asking price from £17,000 to £12,500 in the hope of finding someone looking for an end of season bargain. This proved to be a good move because it produced a purchaser in mid October and several serious enquiries to act as 'back up' in case the original deal fell through.

In spite of our long period of ownership, we were both pleased to see the boat go at last, for somebody else to look after. Peggy was particularly pleased, because although she was still her usual robust, cheerful and busy self, she did find that she was suffering from slowly increasing breathlessness and was still plagued by a persistent cough that all the efforts of our sympathetic doctor failed to cure. It was just as well that by the end of the year both our dogs died; Ike quite quickly, followed by Skip some months later who became so old and slow that he even lost his appetite, requiring us to have him reluctantly, but mercifully put to sleep. By this time, Peggy who had been an enthusiastic dogwalker for hours on end, found that a few hundred yards of walking required a rest to "get her breath back", so that if the dogs had survived, she would not have been able to enjoy walking them as in the past.

Without realising it at the time, the tempo of our lives was slowing imperceptibly with every passing week. On reflection, probably best likened to the slow movement of a Beethoven symphony. The measured rhythm kept its regular slow pace. Many of the complications and worries of our lifestyle had now gone. We were closer and in many ways happier in each other's company than we had been when the tempo of life had been so much quicker just a few years before. The simile of the Beethoven slow movement goes further. The broad sweeps of his melody encompass such beauty, serenity, some sadness and so much nostalgia that it would have been an appropriate, if unheard, background music to the events of the Autumn and Winter of 1995. Sometimes the holding of a hand, with a meeting of eyes and a long gentle smile would say more than a chapter of writing. Peggy, who had scant toleration of television, because of its waste of time, spent increasing hours watching the video recording of Jane Austen's *Pride and Prejudice*. She loved all the characters, the costumes and the music. I am sure she fell in love with Darcy who was able to fulfil, in fiction, the many failings that I brought to her as a husband.

In one way, to my eternal gratitude, I did not fail as she became increasingly unwell. The proximity of Christmas had become a source of worry to her. She made Christmas cakes and other treats to take with us to her brother John's house at Newlyn, where we had been invited, as we took it in turns to share Christmas in each other's houses. That problem she coped with happily and efficiently.

It just so happened that, after Christmas, Boxing Day was going to be our fortieth wedding anniversary. For years past we had always put on a party on Boxing Day for our many friends. For our Ruby Wedding anniversary, Peggy began to agonise over what should be done and how, in her increasingly debilitated state, she would be able to cope with it. I was able to come up with just the right answer:

"You are not fit to cope with the worry and organization of a Boxing Day party. We can have a quiet family celebration of the day with brother John at Newlyn. We will then, as soon as we can, go for a couple of weeks' holiday in the sun on an island we have never visited before, for example, Crete, Cyprus or Madeira."

Peggy raised no objection to this plan, but she did say

"You organize it and I'll go along with it", half expecting that that would be the last she heard of it.

I chose Madeira, having gathered that its relaxed pro British atmosphere, its beautiful scenery and flowers and its lack of appeal to young beach seeking families and the lager lout culture would suit our requirements best. We could not have chosen a better last holiday together. We enjoyed luxurious accommodation beyond what we had anticipated from the travel brochure. We enjoyed taxi trips around the island with a local character called Herculano, who had chauffeured other members of Peggy's family around the island in the past.

We enjoyed the food, the wine, the scenery and the friendship of other people staying at the same waterfront hotel. Although necessarily short, our walks to the shops, the gardens and the restaurants were very happy. When the time came to leave we bought an extravagantly large bunch of orchids, specially boxed for the flight back, because orchids had always been a rare, but special treat for important occasions.

We knew we had to face a visit to the cancer clinic when we returned to Plymouth, because Peggy's consultant wanted to "discuss the latest X Rays." Peggy also had to face a bronchoscopy inspection of her lungs under local anaesthetic, which is a most unpleasant experience.

Within three days of our return, these hurdles had all been crossed. The consultant said the X rays showed a setback, but a regime of hormone treatment and chemotherapy could keep the problem in check. One day later and Peggy needed help to get downstairs for breakfast, after enjoying a reasonably good night's sleep.

The next morning, after telling me what a good night's sleep she had enjoyed, she collapsed halfway down the stairs, struggling desperately for breath. As she held on to the bannister rails to avoid falling down the stairs, I rang for an ambulance.

Before it arrived she died in my arms.

Family, friends and myself were all devastated by the suddenness of her departure. We did, however, have the consolation of knowing that she was spared a long regime of cancer treatment, without any hope of a cure at the end.

In the crowded chapel of the crematorium a few days later, her coffin carried the bunch of orchids, still fresh, brought with such joy from Madeira just a few days before.

On my first visit to Scilly after the funeral, I was able to place in the local magazine *'Scilly Up To Date'* the following notice, which would help to inform Peggy's many friends of what had happened. Many people already knew and were sympathetic towards me as we met in the streets or the shops in Hugh Town. Many others, as I could soon tell from their faces, had not heard of Peggy's death. This magazine is widely read by the Islanders, especially in the quiet Winter season, so it seemed to be the ideal way to spread the news gently around.

From Peggy

Do not be sad for me, but smile,
A robust sense of humour was my style.
I'll be beside you, though you may not see or feel
Me walking Scilly with you, with the dogs at heel.

And when boating around the Islands, still enjoy the wind and spray,
Heading homewards, tired but happy with the magic of the day.

At evening, by the harbour, sitting on your favourite stone,
As the red sun sinks on Samson, you'll never really be alone."

In memory of Peggy who died at home in Plymouth in January '96, having visited Scilly nearly forty times in the last forty nine years.

Finale

A Beethoven slow movement is always followed by an 'upbeat' movement. While Peggy was alive we evolved a philosophy for dealing with life's inevitable problems. Firstly confront them logically and discuss them. Secondly, if the problem proved insoluble at the time, forget about it; worry solves nothing. Thirdly, if there is a strategy for dealing with a problem, get on with it quickly and vigorously.

As soon as the funeral was over I confronted problem number one: as I could no longer justify running two properties, one on the Tamar and one in Scilly, I must choose which to keep and which to sell: no problem. The Tamarside house was too big, with the beach, quay and workshop no longer necessary now that *Fairwater* had been sold. Scilly on the other hand offered a simple flat, big enough for myself and my mother, where we could be surrounded by friends and where we would be away from the hassle and increasing levels of crime in the city of Plymouth.

Most people know of the difficulties of selling a house and moving into another. In my case these were increased because of the accumulation of possessions over forty years of married life and the need to sort these out and then transport them (a) by land to Penzance (b) by sea to St Mary's harbour quay and finally (c) to a new home in the Isles of Scilly.

However pleasant as a holiday flat *Lower Ganilly* lacked a separate granny-flat for my mother and was too small to accommodate my treasured belongings from Plymouth. A simple strategy would be (a) sell the home in Plymouth, (b) move temporarily to *Lower Ganilly*, with the furniture in store somewhere, (c) use the money from the sale of the Plymouth house to buy somewhere desirable in Scilly and then (d) move into a new house in Scilly and sell the flat to put some funds back into the bank balance.

In spite of all my efforts to hasten this process along, it took almost a year to achieve. Good fortune followed the move. My first choice of a new home in Scilly was huge, dilapidated and expensive, but full of future possibilities. In spite of all my best efforts to acquire it, I failed.

Then, from our long-standing, dogwalking friend from Lamerton, near Plymouth, Judith Pengelly, came a cutting from a *Country Living* magazine for a granite cottage for sale at Old Town, St Mary's. I lost no time viewing it, offering a price for it and buying it. My most treasured possessions would fit into it and it had a 'studio flat' which would accommodate my mother. It sat in a third of an acre of garden with granite hedges, it was only a minute's walk from Old Town Harbour and it had a view across to Old Town churchyard where Peggy's ashes had been laid to rest. It had a large workshop in the garden where my woodworking tools from Plymouth would find a happy home. It had rooms where my friends from the Mainland could come down and stay.

As soon as I came in through the granite walled porch and walked through the rooms of the original cottages with their twenty seven inch thick solid granite walls, I felt an atmosphere of welcome, which all subsequent visitors have enjoyed.

I am sure that it is visited by a friendly ghost from Old Town Churchyard and I am sure the ghost approves wholeheartedly of my new home. The previous owner of Bay Tree Cottage told me of a strange experience which he and his dog felt late in the evening of the day on which he accepted my offer for the property:

Visitation

At the back of Bay Cottage the granite rocks stand
And the view past the Bay to the Church they command
And deep in the granite the ley lines lead true
To where in the churchyard they link up with you.

Before there was Church there was still Holy Ground
Where the love of the Celts for their dead could be found
There your ashes still lie 'twixt the Church and the sea
Where you sigh in the surf as you wait there for me.

What joy when you join me in my house made of stone:
While love seeps through the granite I'm never alone.
From the lawns past the Bay, its easy to see
How short is the distance between you and me.

How welcome you were to appear and advise,
Though your spirit's invisible to human eyes.
But I know you were there on the day that I bought
Bay Cottage, the home that I always have sought.

That evening the owner's dog sat at your feet,
Pleased to be able the new ghost to greet
And his big friendly eyes just followed you around
As you came to the cottage without any sound

And he loved you for coming as he "sat and stayed"
While his owner's commands he just disobeyed.
While you walked round the room, to the owner's surprise
The dog sat and looked at you with love in his eyes.

You approved of the room, but as always you planned
An improvement or two which I must take in hand
For you wanted a table in circular style:
For guests in a circle would give you a smile.

So I'll find you that table and I'll find the best
So unfulfilled wishes can then go to rest
And when friends come to dine on the wine and the meat
I'll always make sure that you have your own seat.

And when the meal's over and dogs go to rest,
I know you'll return to the Isles of the Blessed
And gently the room will be filled with the sigh
Of the sea on the sand in the place where you lie.

And so, with my Island friends around me and a couple of boats with which to visit the much loved Off Islands and with my granite cottage by the Old Town harbour, I complete my Odyssey from Tamar to Scilly.

After all the voyaging; after the sun, the gales and the rain; after the calms and the storms; after the excitement, the fear and the sense of achievement when coming into harbour; I am now firmly moored in the haven where I always wished to be.

I am come home.

August 1997.